TERRAPIN
TALES

TERRAPIN TALES

Scott McBrien with Dennis McKay

TERRAPIN TALES

iUniverse books may be ordered through booksellers or by contacting:

iUniverse
1663 Liberty Drive
Bloomington, IN 47403
www.iuniverse.com
1-800-Authors (1-800-288-4677)

Because of the dynamic nature of the Internet, any web addresses or links contained in this book may have changed since publication and may no longer be valid. The views expressed in this work are solely those of the author and do not necessarily reflect the views of the publisher, and the publisher hereby disclaims any responsibility for them.

Any people depicted in stock imagery provided by Thinkstock are models, and such images are being used for illustrative purposes only.
Certain stock imagery © Thinkstock.

ISBN: 978-1-5320-0644-9 (sc)
ISBN: 978-1-5320-0645-6 (e)

Library of Congress Control Number: 2016914734

Print information available on the last page.

iUniverse rev. date: 10/05/2016

ACKNOWLEDGMENTS

Photos of Scott McBrien playing for the University of Maryland were contributed by Mike McNally, Jeff Fishbein, University of Maryland Archives, and University of Maryland Athletic Media Relations.

Preface

I have known Scott McBrien and his family for years. My wife attended grade school with Scott's mother, Kathy, and I have known Scott's uncle, Joe Morris, since high school at Walter Johnson in Bethesda, Maryland, where we were teammates on the baseball team.

Two years ago, Scott asked me to assist him in writing a book about his journey from youth football with Maplewood in Bethesda, Maryland, to starring for the University of Maryland as a standout quarterback in 2002 and 2003.

Through his story, Scott wanted to show to high school athletes in the Washington, DC, Metro area—many of whom, like Scott, grew up rooting for the Terps—the thrill of wearing their hometown school colors and performing before their families and friends.

At first I was hesitant about writing a nonfiction book, since I had only written fiction, but I decided that this was an opportunity to learn a new genre of writing and at the same time tell a good story.

During our first meeting at my house, which I tape-recorded, we worked out a game plan of weekly meetings, with me asking questions, starting when Scott first began organized sports at age seven.

After our first meeting, I sat at my computer, turned on the recorder, and began writing the narrative. By the time we got to Scott's high school and collegiate careers, I began researching his game stats on the Internet. I asked Scott questions about certain game situations, skill sets of teammates and opponents, and his relationships with his coaches and teammates, including some laugh-out-loud incidents.

We met over the course of a year, and over that time a compelling story unfolded, not only about a football career but also about a player's struggle in the competitive, dog-eat-dog world of NCAA football.

Terrapin Tales tells the story of a gifted, yet at times uncertain, player and young man. With the unfailing encouragement of those closest to him, Scott McBrien overcame adversity and won not only in the game of football but also in the game of life.

Dennis McKay
July 11, 2016

Maplewood 75 pound team, 1991

CHAPTER 1

MAPLEWOOD FOOTBALL

My life took a sharp turn in November 1984 when my father moved out of our home in Gaithersburg, Maryland. I was four years old. My little sister Katie was ten months old. Fortunately, my capable mother, Kathy McBrien, had a full-time job, and we were able to stay in the house. At first it seemed strange no longer having my father living with us, but at such a young age I quickly adapted to living in a single-parent household and spending Saturdays with my father.

Another softer and more welcome change occurred in March 1988 when my mother decided to rent our house and move us into my grandmother's place in Kensington, which was thirteen miles to the south and not far from Washington, DC. It was a win-win situation since my beloved grandfather Douglas Morris had recently passed; it would provide my grandmother Mary with company and my mother another adult to help raise Katie and me.

Our new house was a four-bedroom two-story rambler at the end of a dead-end street directly behind White Flint Shopping Center. During the first week in my new home, my grandmother asked my uncle Mike to install a basketball hoop and backboard at the end of the street.

"Your granddad put a hoop up right in this spot in 1958," Uncle Mike said to me as he sunk a posthole digger into a gravelly patch of dirt. "Six Morris kids banged balls off it for over twenty years until one day the whole shebang fell over." He smiled at the memory. "Your grandma said it was the best babysitter she ever had."

What a thrill it was to have my own basketball hoop right in front of my new home. Sometimes Grandma would come out and shoot hoops with me, dressed in her around-the-house outfit of tennis shoes, sweat pants, and a cotton shirt. If that wasn't enough, she would pitch a Wiffle ball to me in the spacious, level backyard. I loved whacking that plastic ball until the day I hit a hard shot back at my grandmother, shattering her glasses. I panicked and ran out of the yard and hid in a neighbor's bushes.

Later, I peeked into the kitchen, where my grandmother was peeling potatoes at the sink. Her broken glasses sat on the counter. She turned to me and smiled, with a bright red mark above her eyebrow. "Where did you go, Scott?" she said as she wiped her hands on a dish towel.

"I got scared, Grandma, when I hit you," I said.

"Oh, honey," she said with a shake of her head, "that was nothing."

I soon understood that Mary Morris let little stop her as she managed the house and all the cooking for her new housemates and continued to organize and celebrate holiday meals for her six children, their spouses, her sixteen grandchildren, and any family friend who had nowhere to go. The more the merrier.

Grandma's home was only a couple of blocks away from my grade school. My mother worked nearby at the National Institute of Health, and since kindergarten, she had been dropping me off and picking me up at Holy Cross School. This made the transition easier for her and also for me since I liked my second-grade teacher, my classmates, and—most of all—recess, when we played sports according to the season: touch football and soccer in the autumn, basketball in the winter, and baseball in the spring. Even at eight years old, I was blessed with quickness and speed and an uncanny ability to throw a ball—any type of ball—with a coordinated, accurate motion.

Though I enjoyed all sports, baseball was my game. During my first summer at my grandmother's, I joined a machine-pitch Little League team, and I was a natural, stealing bases, running down and catching any fly ball I could get my mitt on, and later on I developed into a southpaw pitcher with good speed, pinpoint control, and a devastating three-finger changeup. Throughout my Little League pitching career, few kids could hit me.

Within a couple of weeks of moving into my new home, my best friend, Brian Daly, would often come over to the house after school.

Brian was the biggest kid in the class and by far the most physically mature. Yeah, he was one of those guys.

Brian and I would shoot hoops or take turns hitting and fielding with my grandmother—who Brian called Grandma—pitching the Wiffle ball to us. Afterward, my grandmother served us our go-to treat of sliced bananas with milk and sugar sprinkled on top.

In a pinch, Grandma's house became an after-school hangout spot for my friends at Holy Cross. For instance, when soccer practice ended early, some kids would walk home with me, and we'd play a quick game of Wiffle ball and then scurry into the kitchen for a freshly baked batch of chocolate chip cookies before their parents picked them up.

My friends soon followed Brian's lead and began calling my grandmother Grandma, as did some of their parents. Everyone loved Mary Morris, a short, white-haired Irish lass with a sturdy yet trim figure and one of those smiles that makes everyone upon whom it shines feel welcomed.

The following fall, Brian talked me into trying out for his flag football team, which was affiliated with the Wheaton Boys Club. After the first day of practice, I told my mother that I would never go back. Although a flag league, there was full contact, and we played in shoulder pads. Blocking and hard hits were part of the game, and I didn't like it. I kept telling myself that I was a baseball player. She convinced me to continue, but after every practice I felt like quitting.

Before the first game, I sat with my mother and father—who attended most of my games—on a hill overlooking the field, and I refused to join my teammates for warm-ups. I sat there, and sat there, and sat there, never joining them. I sat on that hill and watched the whole first half as a spectator. By the beginning of the second half, my parents had convinced me to join my teammates, and the coach put me right in. I ended up running two kickoffs back for touchdowns. Even so, I didn't like football and quit after the game.

By the spring of 1990, I was immersed in Little League baseball and organized football was a long-ago memory. My parents, Katie, and sometimes my grandmother would sit in the bleachers behind our bench cheering my team on. When I wasn't pitching, I was playing center field or hitting the daylights out of the ball. Baseball came easily to me—very easily.

Then everything changed that summer at Bethany Beach, Delaware, where the Morris clan vacationed every year. I was throwing a football on the beach with my good friend Jamie Hart when his father, Bret, saw me throwing tight, accurate spirals. Bret asked my mother if I would be interested in joining Jamie in the fall to play Maplewood Football, which was a member of an organized football league for ages six through fourteen. Since Jamie was playing, I said I would give it a try.

But my mother had begun having second thoughts about me playing a contact sport. I was small for my age, and she worried that I could get hurt playing tackle football. She finally relented when I fell off my bike and received twelve stitches on my chin. "See Mom," I told her on the way back from the emergency room, "I can get hurt anywhere."

Maplewood home games and practices were held at Alta Vista Park, located in an upper-middle-class neighborhood in Bethesda. It was an idyllic spot, with a playground, tennis and basketball courts, and a baseball backstop and dirt infield tucked into a corner of the wide, long field. Pickup basketball games and tennis matches competed simultaneously with the organized yet chaotic scene of swarms of boys in football gear scrimmaging, shouts of encouragement rising and falling through the late summer air, and the smell of dust and sweat filling our nostrils. It seemed as though a contagious energy had swept over the park, infecting anyone in the vicinity.

All the different teams, from peewees up to 110 pounds, crammed onto the field every day after school, with the parents—mostly fathers—watching and a few mothers with little ones in tow. Many of the dads had played football in high school, others in college, and they all kept a close eye on their sons as they lined up in rows during jumping jacks and up-downs.

After warm-ups, the offense ran plays against the defense. The crack of linemen colliding shoulder pad to shoulder pad and the barked instructions of coaches, on both sides of the ball, echoed across the field: "Block with shoulders square, back straight," and "Wrap up and drive into the ball carrier."

Already tired, we finished practice straining and grunting through a series of lung-choking wind sprints up the hill on the side of the field. After wind sprints, each team huddled around their coaches for a breakdown of practice.

Chief was the name of my first Maplewood coach on the 75-pound Pony A team. I had played up an age group in order to play with Jamie. I asked Chief if I could play quarterback, but he told me the position was filled.

I ended up as a third-string tailback—not what I had imagined. The starting quarterback was a kid named Marc Roberge, who went on to become the lead singer for a major rock band named O.A.R. Our tailbacks were a pair of shifty runners named Keith Urgo and Devon Tuohey. Not many kids could tackle either one in the open field. Looking back on it now, what probably kept me from giving up on football for good was that whenever Chief needed a big play, he would put me in for the "Chief's Play"—a halfback option. I would line up at tailback, and Marc would pitch the ball to me on a sweep to the left. It always surprised the defense when I cocked my left arm and threw the ball thirty yards down the field to tight end Andrew Toussaint on a deep crossing route. It was a new and exciting feeling to connect on a big play like that. So were the camaraderie and the roar of the crowd.

The following season, I remained on the 75-pound A team to play with my own age group and was coached by my uncle Joe Morris and his best friend, Pat Meyers, who was a close family friend and like another uncle to me. Uncle Joe drove me to and from practice every day after school. I didn't have a father around, but both Uncle Joe and Pat helped fill the void.

Their quarterback coach that year remains a good friend to this day. Joe LaPietra had moved to the Washington, DC, area a few years after graduating from Franklin & Marshall, where he had played quarterback.

Uncle Joe and Pat knew little about quarterback play. Fortuitously, Joe LaPietra stopped by the first day of practice and asked Pat if he needed any coaching help. So they brought Joe on as the quarterback coach and offensive coordinator. It was a good move. He taught me the fundamentals of quarterback play: speak loud and clear in the huddle and look my teammates in the eye; after receiving the snap from center, keep my elbows close to my body; when dropping back to pass, position the ball high and close to my chest; on a run play, look the ball or fake into a ball carrier's belly. And Joe told me over and over again, "Carry out the play fake around the end like you have possession of the ball." Then when I did keep the ball, by the time the defense figured it out, I would be running in open space. "Get that defensive end to bite, Scott," Joe would tell me, "and we have a big play on our hands."

My first meeting with Joe is something he still kids me about. I had reported a week late to camp because I had been at Bethany Beach with my family. At first, Joe didn't want to let me run with the first team since I hadn't shown up on time. But Uncle Joe and Pat both told him that I was their quarterback. "Watch him throw the ball, Joe," Pat told him, "and you'll see."

Joe held his ground, keeping me on the bench for a couple of series before waving me into the huddle. I knew I had to impress this young coach, and I began firing bullets to the receivers, hitting them in stride on play after play. After that there was no more talk about me not starting. I was beginning to understand that talent made up for a lot of things.

Besides my learning experiences as a football player, I was becoming immersed in the Maplewood community, and I had three coaches who treated me like one of their own. We were all in it together. Hail, Maplewood!

And we had the *sweetest* white uniforms with numerals on the chest and shoulders and maple leafs on the upper sleeves—all in a rich blue—and white helmets with a maple leaf insignia.

The games were so different from baseball, which were played in front of a handful of parents. Maplewood Football drew good crowds, including parents, grandparents, former players, and Alta Vista neighborhood folks interested in little league football.

We played on Saturday, so my mother and Katie attended every game. When Grandma came, they would situate themselves away from the hubbub, on a little rise past the end zone, Grandma sitting in a lawn chair, Katie and my mother standing on either side of her.

We even had a mouthwatering barbeque, compliments of one of the fathers, Miller Young, who lived in the neighborhood and towed his smoker to home games. All of this contributed to an air of excitement, as though waiting for something to explode. Maplewood Football was taking hold of my life.

And so was the competition, especially against our biggest rival, the always tough Wheaton Boys Club coached by James White, who was as flashy as it got, dressed in a sleek all-red tracksuit with a ball cap worn backward. Coach White constantly talked during games, either to his players or the refs. "Watch number ten on the quarterback option. Look out, here it comes!" and "Hey, Ref, the left defensive end is jumping the gun. There he goes!" The man was a ball of energy.

Wheaton was a working-class neighborhood that bred tough people who bred tough kids, and Coach White always found a way to put together great teams known for their talented tailbacks and hard hits.

During my second 75-pound season against Wheaton, we were in a knock 'em, sock 'em contest. With ten seconds left in the game, we had possession of the ball on the fifty yard line, down by somewhere around a touchdown. There was no scoreboard, so during games my teammates and I were never quite sure what the score was. We had an idea but never knew the exact score unless a coach told us. I just knew we were down by seven points or less.

Whenever we needed a big play, Joe LaPietra would move me from quarterback to tailback, move John Conroy from tight end to quarterback, and call either sweep right or sweep left. I never understood why other coaches couldn't figure out a way to stop me on a simple sweep, but they never did. And for whatever reason, John Conroy would one-hop the sweep pitch to me every single time, so I would have to scoop up the ball, gather myself, and head for the end zone—the true meaning of a scoop and score.

Coach LaPietra called the pitch play to the right. Conroy pitched me a one-hopper. I scooped it up and took off with nothing but open space and the end zone ahead of me. I had a walk-in touchdown, except that when I got to the ten yard line I started to stumble. If I fell before the end zone, the play and the game would be over, and we would lose. Somehow I managed to stumble forward to the three yard line, and as I was falling, I dove and stretched out over the goal line for a touchdown.

I ran toward the sidelines with my arms raised over my head, screaming at the top of my lungs. Uncle Joe picked me up, threw me over his shoulder, and ran along the sideline, clutching me like a sack of potatoes.

"You need to kick the extra point, Scott," Uncle Joe said as he plopped me down.

"Did we win?" I said.

"The game is over, and we won by a point," Uncle Joe said. "But we need to go through the formality of kicking the extra point."

In youth football, if you decided to kick the ball through the uprights for the point after a touchdown, it counted as two points since kicking extra points at that age level was difficult. I was the kicker and made most of our extra points, but even so, I felt no pressure since my uncle had told me we had already won the game. I kicked the ball through the uprights, but it turned out we had been down by a point before the kick, so we won the game by a point!

After every game, I would go to our halfback Jon Neal's house to watch the game we'd just played, which Jon's dad, Jack, had filmed and commentated. Mr. Neal did this for every game Jon and I played in for four seasons straight.

Jon and I couldn't wait to watch the Wheaton game, and the film didn't let us down. On my game-winning run, Mr. Neal's commentary was classic: "The Franchise is around the corner, the Franchise is in the clear, the Franchise drives into the end zone. The Franchise has struck once again."

After my mother picked me up from Jon's house, we would head over to Pat Meyers's house, which was only a few blocks from my grandmother's, and join the coaches and their families for a barbeque cookout.

Pat lived on Bangor Drive, and everyone at Maplewood called his house Club Bangor. It was a great place for the adults to forget about the daily grind as they drank a cold beer or a glass of wine while Pat manned the grill, flipping burgers with one hand and holding a cold Budweiser in the other.

Club Bangor was kid friendly, with an assortment of video games in the rec room and a basketball backboard out front where I'd shoot hoops with Pat's two boys, Scott and Sean, and my Uncle Joe's son, Jake.

Over the course of the evening, the coaches would rehash the game, passing cold beers all around, laughing, and having a good old time. I always knew when Pat was about to compliment me on a play: "Scoottt," he would say in a deep rumbly voice, "great throw on third down to Kent Young on that fade pattern." Pat was a big-shouldered, heavy-set man with a shock of sandy red hair and gregarious way about him. Even when he was chewing a player out, there was a ring of affection in his voice.

During these gatherings, there was an air of excitement and good cheer. Some of my best memories were at Club Bangor.

In the world of Maplewood Football, my talent as a quarterback presented opportunities and status that otherwise would not have been available to me, and though I never showed it, I basked in it.

Over the years, I pulled off a few more last-minute, come-from-behind victories against Wheaton, and Coach White nicknamed me the Wheaton Killer. To this day, Coach White and I still stay in touch via e-mail. That is the type of respect we had for each other, he as a coach and me as a player.

But I almost never acquired the Wheaton Killer moniker. By the time I was to join the 95-pound team, I didn't show up for the first practice. I did not get along with the head coach, who had coached me the previous season on the 85-pound team. Joe LaPietra got word that I hadn't attended practice, and he came over to my grandmother's house with my Maplewood jersey and handed it to me.

Joe LaPietra told me that the coach of the 95-pound team wanted me to have it. I looked at the white jersey with the number ten on the front and back and shoulders and the maple leafs on both arms—all in that beautiful blue. I loved that uniform. I loved Maplewood. But still I said to Joe, "I'm not playing for him. All he does is yell at me."

We were in the kitchen, and Joe exchanged a look with my grandmother, who was preparing dinner at the stove. Her eyes seemed to say to Joe, *Do what you have to do, but get him playing ball.*

Joe took me out into the backyard and we sat down, face-to-face, in lawn chairs. Joe had a passionate intensity about him, and when Joe LaPietra talked, I listened.

It was broiling hot outside. The sun was beating down on us, and I felt like a witness about to get grilled by the prosecuting attorney.

"Scott," Joe said as he wiped a bead of sweat off his forehead and leaned forward, hands on knees, squinting, "you're going to face obstacles throughout your life and every time things get difficult you need to work your way through it." Joe made a face. *Understand.* "You have a unique talent in this game," he said as he eased back in his chair, "but it will only take you so far if you don't have the stick-with-it quality that is needed to succeed, not just in football but in life."

Of course, now I look back at myself and realize how fortunate I was to have someone like Joe LaPietra to steer me in the right direction. I also realized that, once again, my talent for football had given me a second chance that other kids might not have been given. If I had been a second-string tackle, would anyone have even bothered with me?

During the 95-pound season, Bret Hart, who had been an assistant coach at the University of Maryland back in the '70s, would take Jamie, me, and some of our Maplewood teammates out to College Park to watch the Maryland football team play.

All we heard about was a former Maplewood player named Kevin Plank who played linebacker and special teams for Maryland. Before the start of games, we would run down to the front row of Byrd Stadium wearing our Maplewood jerseys and yelling for Kevin, who would come up to us, high-fiving and tossing out wrist bands. We loved it. Of course, little did we know that Kevin Plank would go on to become CEO and founder of Under Armour, one of the largest manufacturers of sports performance apparel, footwear, and accessories in the world.

The 95-pound team ended up playing in the championship game at Byrd Stadium. Maplewood lost the game, but I will never forget stepping into the Maryland team locker room—the smell of liniment and perspiration lingering in the air, the tall lockers, and the big-boy benches—and playing in a major college football stadium. The grass on the field was heaven and seemed like a fairway at Augusta compared to some of the dust bowls we had played on during the season. At that point in time, it hit me that I wanted to be a Maryland Terrapin and play in front of a large Division 1 home crowd in College Park.

As it turned out, I was not the only one with aspirations of me playing Division 1. Shortly after the Maplewood season ended, I was downstairs in the den shooting pool when Uncle Joe came through the front door, waved me a hello, and scooted up the steps. It was unusual for Joe not to spend at least a minute talking to me, so I figured something was up.

The den was situated below the kitchen, and if I put my ear near the wall, I could overhear a conversation.

"Kathy," Joe said, "Scott has the ability to earn a scholarship to play Division 1 football."

Whoa, I thought, *Joe knows sports, and if he says it, it must be true.*

"Really?" my mother said with a rise in her voice. She then said something I couldn't make out, and Joe said, "But, at five feet two and ninety-five pounds, Scott is small for his age. What do you think if he stayed back a year so by the time he graduates high school, he would have an extra year of growth."

At this point, I almost tore up the steps and shouted, "No way! Absolutely no way!" I did not want to have to repeat eighth grade, especially when I didn't have to.

My mother said, "Funny you should mention this, Joe. I was thinking he doesn't seem emotionally or physically mature enough for high school."

There was silence as I imagined the two of them looking at each other as if to say, *Dare we do this?*

Joe told her he had to run but to think about it.

I decided not to say anything to my mother, who would have been mad at me for eavesdropping, and hoped she would let me go on to high school.

Repeating eighth grade was put on the back burner when I won the Timmie Award for Local Schoolboy Player of the Year, and I was asked to give an acceptance speech in front of three thousand people at the Hilton Hotel in Washington, DC. I was thirteen years old and had never given a speech before, let alone at a black-tie dinner ceremony in front of famous athletes, national politicians, and even some Hollywood celebrities.

The awards banquet was put on by the Washington DC Touchdown Club, which was started in 1935, and it honored high school, college, and professional athletes of all sports across the country. This was a big deal. *Sports Illustrated* magazine had called it "the granddaddy of all sports banquets."

I was nervous about speaking at such an event, but once again Joe LaPietra came to my rescue. He not only helped me write the speech, but he drove me to his office and had me rehearse in front of his colleagues. I practiced that speech for over a month and knew it inside and out.

Joe had become a surrogate big brother and someone who would pick me up and drive me to games, just the two of us talking not just about the upcoming game but sports or what it was like as a kid growing up *back in the day*. He told me that the reason he coached at Maplewood was because his father told him he needed to give back to the community the way other men had done for him when he was playing ball as a boy.

The day before the event, a couple of buses drove all the award winners from the Hilton, where my mother and I had been put up for two nights, to a lunch banquet at the Washington DC Touchdown Club on K Street.

Sitting at the back of the bus was Heath Shuler, the star quarterback from the University of Tennessee, who would go on to be drafted in the first round by the Washington Redskins. Joe LaPietra was sitting next to me, and he told me we were going to walk back and meet Heath. I was apprehensive, not sure if I would be bothering him or if he might blow me off.

Joe introduced me as Schoolboy Player of the Year and a left-handed quarterback. Heath looked huge to me. He was a broad-shouldered, handsome young man who looked every bit the All-SEC quarterback he was.

Heath grimaced a smile and told me I was on the wrong side of the ball. "No left-handed quarterbacks where I come from, boy." Maybe he was kidding, but I didn't take it that way and walked away thinking, *Who is this cocky guy to tell me I can't play quarterback?* Not the best way to begin the festivities.

During the luncheon, the other athlete at my table was the Collegiate Golfer of the Year. I was more than a little disappointed that I hadn't gotten a chance to sit with one of the star athletes in attendance like Barry Bonds, Rod Woodson, Art Monk, or Paul Molitor. Little did I know that my tablemate would turn out to be an all-time great by the name of Tiger Woods, who even back then had an aura of confidence about him. The event didn't seem too big for him.

The next night at the awards dinner, Joe spotted Trent Dilfer, who was also a college quarterback and would go on to win a Super Bowl with the Baltimore Ravens. "Come on, Scott," Joe said, lifting his chin toward Trent, "another quarterback for you to meet."

I was nervous as all get-out about giving a speech, and now Joe wanted me to meet another college star. Joe gave his spiel to Trent, who was even bigger than Heath Shuler, about me winning the Timmie Award and being a lefty quarterback.

Trent was the opposite of Shuler. He shook my hand firmly and told me it was great to meet me. Trent told me that being a lefty quarterback was unique and offered a different look for the defense. "Sort of like a lefty pitcher in baseball," he said with a nod. He offered to have a picture taken of us together in our tuxedos—a very cool moment for a thirteen-year-old kid.

Later, I bumped into Heath, and this time he was as nice as could be. "There's the little lefty," he said through a big smile. He even posed for a picture with me. To this day, I wonder if I misconstrued his attitude toward me on the bus and he'd really just been having fun with me.

During my speech, I spoke from the heart about what a great family I had, especially my mother and grandmother, in supporting me on and off the field. I mentioned by name the coaches who had contributed to my advancement as a football player and as a person, and then I said that football was a team sport and without all of my teammates I would not have been standing there that evening. In conclusion, I thanked the Touchdown Club and congratulated the other award winners.

As I left the dais, the room erupted in a standing ovation. I was stunned and then stunned twice more. The first was when NFL Hall of Famer Merlin Olsen, who was the emcee, kiddingly said I would be spending the summer giving seminars to professional athletes on how to accept awards, which was followed by another round of applause. And later on, Barry Bonds mentioned during his acceptance speech that he hoped his kids would grow up to be just like me and that I was a role model for every youth athlete out there. The following week, George Michaels, the sports anchor for the NBC affiliate in the Washington, DC, area, raved on air about the superb speech given by young Scott McBrien.

But my thinking that winning the Timmie Award and all the accolades that came with it would sway my mother to allow me to go to one of the three Catholic high schools—Georgetown Prep, Good Counsel, and DeMatha—I had applied to was nixed when she and Uncle Joe sat me down in the kitchen and laid out their plan for me to get a scholarship to a Division 1 school.

I tried to talk them out of it, but my mother was adamant that I was going to repeat eighth grade. "It's for the best, Scott," she said.

Most of my friends from Holy Cross School and Maplewood Football were heading on to high school, and here I was repeating eighth grade at Mater Dei School, a private Catholic school in Potomac, Maryland, known for its academics.

I had hoped to attend Georgetown Prep, having grown up a few blocks away. Prep was one of the oldest all-boys schools in the country and was steeped in tradition. Situated on ninety acres, it had a stately Ivy League atmosphere with brick arches, gabled dormers, a portico, a lovely chapel, and even a field house. I liked everything about the school, especially the football games: the sound of the beating single drum, the cheering student section, and the aura of camaraderie about the place.

But when Prep rejected me, they suggested I repeat eighth grade at Mater Dei and reapply next year, with the promise of acceptance. That made it easier to accept my mother's decision to stay back a year. At this point I realized that my talent for football was—in my mind—working against me.

After a fun summer of hanging out with friends, playing hoops and touch football, and spending two weeks at Bethany Beach, I reported to Mater Dei in the first week of September. Making the transition easier was the opportunity to play another season at Maplewood on the

110-pound team alongside my good buddy Jamie Hart, who had always played a weight class ahead of me since our first year together.

Jamie had to lose a few pounds to make weight, but he made the cut, and we had a great final season coached by his father, Bret, with the help of Joe LaPietra, who left Uncle Joe and Pat Meyers on the 75-pound team to help coach me at quarterback.

By this time, everyone at Maplewood was aware of my potential as a quarterback. I was athletic and quick, but what set me apart was my left arm that threw an accurate tight spiral. I had a gift that, at the time, I took for granted. I had a lot to learn, not only about football but also about life.

After a successful 110-pound season, my team was invited to play in a weekend tournament down in Gainesville, Florida, against two 150-pound teams. At this point in the season, some of our players weighed over 130-pounds, but there was still a big size advantage for the other teams.

I almost didn't get to make the trip when I came down with strep throat a few days before departure. Coach Hart and Fuzzy Myers—who was commissioner of Maplewood Football—both called my mother and told her she had to do whatever it took to get me ready to play. She told them that if I recovered enough to travel and play, they would need to buy her an airplane ticket to come down and look after me.

I got some bed rest, and though I felt better, I was still a bit under the weather by the time we departed for Florida with my worried mother along to keep an eye on me. After landing, we took an hour ride to our hotel in Gainesville—my first road trip.

If we won the first game on a Friday night, we would advance to a championship game Sunday afternoon. Because of my shaky health, I only played offense and kicked—no defensive back play.

Not only were our opponents from Davie, Florida, huge, but they were loaded with talent. They had two studs at running back that looked like they were starters on their varsity high school teams.

This all-black team was extremely fast and athletic on both sides of the ball. They stopped our running attack with no problem. Their issue was stopping me through the air and covering my go-to receiver, Kevin Brant. I went eight for ten with a touchdown pass to win the game 16–7.

It felt good to get a win under our belts and get a day of rest before our championship game.

The next day at the weigh-in for all the marbles, my Maplewood teammates and I watched as one after another of our opponents—an all-star team from Gainesville—tipped the scale at nearly 150 pounds. They stripped down to practically nothing to make weight.

After a couple of Maplewood boys weighed in with all their pads on and didn't come close to the maximum weight, the other team's coaches said the rest of our team didn't even have to weigh in. That's how confident they were.

Those coaches and their players were in for a shock. Maplewood didn't have the size, but we did have a group of never-say-die teammates and a top-flight coaching staff.

The Gainesville team was loaded with talent. They had huge, athletic players at every position. They looked great in uniform, but I bet they had never faced a team that took it to them physically like we did. We out-hit them early.

On the first drive, we punched them in the mouth, driving right down the field, and went up 6–0; I had a rare miss of an extra point. In the second quarter, we scored again and extended our lead to 14–0 when I converted the extra point kick for two points.

Late in the second quarter, we were leading 14–7, and I was clicking on all cylinders, passing the ball as we drove down to the five yard line with ten seconds left on the clock before halftime. Coach Hart called a time-out and decided that we were going to attempt a pass to the end zone for a touchdown. If it was incomplete, we would kick a field goal and go into halftime up 17–7.

I threw the ball into the back corner of the end zone. One of the few white kids on the opposing team picked it off, tiptoeing to stay in bounds, and ended up taking it all the way back for a 109-yard touchdown. Nobody was catching that kid; he was one of the fastest players I had ever seen at that age. We went into halftime 14–14.

The game went back and forth in the second half, and the heat and humidity was beginning to take a toll on us. The field was a dust bowl, and we were in a dogfight against a larger team that was beginning to wear us down. But we held on, and at the end of regulation, the score was still tied 14–14. Next up, overtime.

Gainesville scored on their first possession from our ten yard line and ran in the extra point to go up by seven points. As I mentioned, back then not many teams had kickers, but little did our opponent know that I converted the extra point kick 95 percent of the time.

Now it was Maplewood's turn. We ran the ball on first down and got stopped. Ran the ball on second down and got stopped again. Third and goal from the ten yard line, I threw a slant pass to Kevin Brant, who was tackled down at the one yard line.

Coach Hart called a time-out.

Fourth and goal from the one yard line, we ran the ball with our tiny but quick tailback, Pat Donnelly, who could fit through any hole the line could create for him. Pat tucked the ball, put his head down, and scored the touchdown. Down by one point, I kicked the extra point through the uprights, and Maplewood won the weekend tournament by one point in overtime.

It was a moment that everyone on that team would take with us for the rest of his life, coaches included. Up to that point, I had never experienced such a total feeling of elation, having beaten a couple of top-flight programs. Florida was and still remains a college recruiting hotbed, and I imagine more than a few of our opponents went on to play for Division 1 college programs.

Maplewood Football was a critical part of my maturation. I'm not sure where I would be today without it. I am so very thankful, not only for the opportunity to play but also for all the friends I made and have kept to this day. And most importantly, I am grateful for the lessons I learned on the field about never-say-die teamwork.

Finally, let me say thank you to all the men who guided and coached me at Maplewood. Without you, I would have never gone on to become the high school, college, or professional athlete I was or the person I am today. Hail, Maplewood!

CHAPTER 2

THE TRANSITION

After the Maplewood season ended, I had to put all my effort into the classroom rigors of Mater Dei. I had developed an anxiety issue: new school, new teachers, new friends, difficult classwork. Mater Dei was a shock academically. I would come home in tears because of the amount of homework each night. There was so much pressure to keep up with my classmates that I felt as if I was going to throw up every day at school. It got so bad that I was declared academically ineligible for the second half of the basketball season for the Mater Dei team because of poor grades. So while my teammates went to practice or a game, I went to study hall.

With a lot of hard work, I got my grades up, and when springtime arrived, it was time to apply to high school again. I had my heart set on attending Georgetown Prep, but my mother insisted that I apply to Good Counsel as a backup.

The letters arrived on the same day, Good Counsel's thick and Prep's thin. I was heartbroken that Georgetown Prep had gone back on their word and turned me down once again. I had stayed back and gone through so much partly to be able to attend Prep, and to me, it seemed like it all had been for nothing.

I opened the Good Counsel packet and I had been accepted. It took about a week for me to get over Prep's rejection, but I had grade school and Maplewood friends attending Good Counsel and I was looking forward to joining them, especially my two childhood best friends, Brian Daly and Jamie Hart. Brian went to Good Counsel after we graduated from Holy Cross Elementary, so he was going into his sophomore year.

As freshmen, Jamie and I were asked by the junior varsity football coaches if we wanted to skip over the freshman team. I was a little nervous at first because of my size. I wasn't so sure that I could compete with all the big kids at 120 pounds soaking wet. But Maplewood Football, and specifically Joe La Pietra, had given me a good education on playing quarterback, and combined with my natural ability to throw the ball, I won the starting quarterback position. Other than the bigger size of my teammates and our JV competition, the complexities of the game and the skill level were not that much more advanced than Maplewood.

That year, our team ended up 5–3, which wasn't a championship season, but we had a blast, and along the way I made friends with a wide variety of kids at Good Counsel.

After the JV season ended, I practiced with the varsity squad and was in uniform for the WCAC (Washington Catholic Athletic Conference) championship game, in our division, against Bishop O'Connell at Byrd Stadium. Once again, my talent provided me with opportunities. I couldn't help but imagine myself on this field in a few years playing for the Terps in front of a packed stadium of fifty-five thousand strong.

We ended up winning the game and becoming WCAC champs. I had come a long way from Maplewood in a short time.

After the football season, I played on the freshman basketball team at point guard, along with fullback/linebacker Josh Ott and linebacker Jamie Hart. We became teammates and friends with our basketball teammates, but the upperclassman on the football team had a way of reminding us that we were football players first.

One afternoon after practice, Josh and I walked a few blocks from school to a Burger King to grab something to eat. As we sat in a booth, waiting for our order, Josh told me that today was his birthday and the upperclassman had given him a series of punches on his arm as a birthday hazing.

"My arm is so sore, I can barely lift it," Josh said, looking up as the front door opened. I will never forget the look of shock on his face. I turned to see four senior linemen making a beeline for Josh—another birthday knock?

Josh tore out of the booth, hand-vaulted over the front counter, raced through the kitchen as workers scattered every which way, and bolted out the back door, never looking back. It was the fastest I had ever seen him move. I would have thought it was funny, except my birthday was the very next day. But either the seniors didn't know or maybe thought I was too small and frail to give a pounding to. More likely, it was because I was a quarterback.

Quarterback was the most important position on the field, and losing a starting quarterback could ruin a season. If the coaches had gotten word that I had been roughed up by a group of older teammates, there would have been hell to pay. For a running back/linebacker like Josh, not so much.

After a summer of working out with friends in the weight room at Georgetown Prep, playing in a touch football league with my Good Counsel teammates, and spending two weeks at Bethany Beach, I reported to football camp at Good Counsel.

I was assigned to the varsity team, and to my surprise, I was competing for the starting quarterback position. By this point, I was in the midst of a growth spurt and had sprouted up to five feet nine, but only weighed 140 pounds. I was unsure if I wanted the pressure of starting quarterback on my shoulders.

But deep down I felt that I could compete at this level; I had the football instincts, the arm, and the background to play in the WCAC. All I had to do was ignore the negative frets and worries that smoldered below the surface. This was new to me, since at Maplewood I'd never had any doubts about my ability to compete.

By the end of training camp, the head coach decided I would split time with a junior at quarterback, and I would be limited to playing in the second and fourth quarters. The first game of the season, we traveled on the Thursday before school started, by bus, all the way down to the southwest corner of Virginia to play Pulaski County High School.

After checking into a local hotel, the team took the bus over to the school. We then went through walk-throughs the night before the game on a football field with a long, deep stretch of bleachers that were bigger than at any high school I had ever seen.

It was like being at a small college. The school was situated on acres of land that had, besides the well-manicured football field, an immaculate baseball diamond, tennis courts—all with lights—and ample parking lots. The school itself was a cluster of brick buildings, everything neat and orderly. And there was an aura about the place that suggested football was taken seriously. Very seriously.

After a night of restless sleep, the game, played under the lights on Friday night, turned out to be a nightmare as they beat us soundly. Pulaski was a well-coached, disciplined team—everything we seemed not to be at that point. In my two quarters of play, I didn't do much, and once again that negative voice crept into my psyche: *You're in over your head. You're too small for all these big-time players.*

The next two games, I continued playing the second and fourth quarter. I was improving little by little as I began to hit my receivers in stride, keep my poise after a mistake, and try to keep an upbeat attitude to encourage my teammates. Despite our 1–2 record, I had a feeling we were coming together as a team.

Before practice the Monday after our third game, the coach named me the permanent starter. Wow! I was excited and scared at the same time. But I soon became comfortable as the starting quarterback, and by our ninth game of the season, we had a 5–3 record and were 4–1 in our division in the WCAC.

Then reality hit. Our next game was against DeMatha at Good Counsel. The DeMatha Stags were a perennial powerhouse program with Division 1 talent all over the field.

Good Counsel hadn't beaten DeMatha in twenty-seven years. In a way, this took the pressure off me. No one expected us to win.

During warm-ups, I was impressed with everything about the DeMatha Stags: the size and athleticism of the players; the way they went through the stretch line with a choreographed rhythm; the manner in which their players confidently carried themselves in their sharp white uniforms with red numerals and leg stripes and *DeMATHA* in blue across their chests; and the coaches dressed in sleek jumpsuits. They had a presence.

Two plays stood out in that game. On the first play from scrimmage, I faked a hand off to the running back and rolled out to my left—just like I had done for years at Maplewood—and hit my tight end Zach Hilton on a deep corner route for a touchdown over Tony Okanlawon, who I would go on to play with at Maryland. I couldn't believe it; we were leading DeMatha 7–0 after one play from scrimmage. That pass gave me the confidence I needed.

After that, it was a back-and-forth contest until we were ahead by two points with under a minute left in the game. But DeMatha had driven the ball down to our one yard line. They were about to punch it in and ice the game. The Stags had a powerful offensive line, and to make matters worse, they had their stud tackle, Marvin Jones lined up at fullback in front of their soon-to-be Ohio State Buckeye tailback, Scott Fulton. It was as though they were saying, *We are going to run this ball down your throat, and there is nothing you can do about it.*

My grandmother had given me a Saint Christopher medal to pin inside my football pants as a good luck charm. I went down to one knee with my hand atop my good luck medal and said a little prayer for a miracle.

My wish became a reality when the quarterback snap was fumbled and our cornerback Eric LaHaie scooped the ball up and ran it back ninety-seven yards for the winning touchdown. After the extra point, we led by nine points. I couldn't believe what I was witnessing.

DeMatha scored a meaningless touchdown right before the final whistle, and we won the game 28–26. On the field, my teammates were shouting and screaming and hugging each other, and from the stands came a roar of approval from our fans that kept growing louder and louder. The miracle on Georgia Avenue had happened. We had just upset the number one team in the state.

I had run the offense smoothly, getting the team in and out of huddles and throwing the ball effectively enough to keep their defense honest. I was now confident that I could not only play in a tough, competitive league like the WCAC, but I could succeed in it. Not bad for a 140-pound lefty in his first varsity season.

The DeMatha win propelled us to go on to a 7–1 league record and qualified us for the WCAC playoffs. I was in my wheelhouse, confident and sure of my ability as a quarterback, which carried over to my status in school and beyond.

On Mondays after wins, students and sometimes teachers would congratulate me before a class or in the hallways between classes. Girls from Walter Johnson High, Holy Cross Academy, and Georgetown

Visitation invited me to their homecoming dances, all three of which I attended, plus Good Counsel's. I maintained an attitude of modest appreciation, but inside I loved every moment of it.

We won the first playoff game 53–13 against Paul VI, with me throwing three touchdown passes and our running back Doug Bost having a field day on the ground. I was now getting quoted in the *Montgomery County Gazette* after games, and I always made sure to compliment the offensive line for giving me time to throw the ball.

Our first playoff win propelled us into the WCAC championship game at none other than Byrd Stadium, where we would face a solid St. Johns squad, which had some talented players, led by their bruising quarterback, Brian Calabrese, who also played linebacker.

I was thrilled to get an opportunity to play once again at Maryland, as I was sure there would be some college scouts at the game, including from Maryland; I was now thinking it actually might be possible to play for the Terps one day. I began to try to see myself as a college recruiter might: *McBrien is a lefty with a strong enough arm, but what stands out is his accuracy and the efficient manner in which he runs an offense. His weakness is his size, but he's only a sophomore and looks as though he still has some growing to do. He is a player worth keeping an eye on as he continues to progress and grow.*

We started off the St. Johns game with me hitting Kenny Gaskins on a slant pass for a touchdown, and after that, my teammates and I were hitting on all cylinders. St. Johns was a strong opponent, but we ruled the day and went on to win the game 39–15. Never in my dreams could I have imagined a better way to start my varsity career: as the quarterback of the WCAC champions.

By the end of November, my Uncle Joe had been talking to my mother about me transferring to DeMatha. Joe thought DeMatha offered me the best opportunity to be seen by college scouts and get an athletic scholarship. I was leery, seeing as how I was the starting quarterback at Good Counsel, where I had a ton of friends and liked everything about the school. Even though I had quarterbacked my team to a win over them, I wasn't sure if I could start at DeMatha. But Uncle Joe mentioned that their starting quarterback was a senior, leaving the door open for me to compete.

I decided to contact Tim Strachan, who was a family friend and had been a star quarterback at DeMatha in the early '90s. Tim had watched me play at Maplewood and Good Counsel, and he thought I had the ability to start at his old school. He told me I would have to compete for the starting job but that I had the arm and football smarts to play at DeMatha. Tim also said, "If you want to play at the next level, Scott, you can't beat DeMatha for providing a great football education."

If I stayed at Good Counsel, would I afford myself the best opportunity for a scholarship to play in college? What if I did leave and transfer to DeMatha? I was happy at Good Counsel and was in the middle of the JV basketball season.

Even though I would be going into a situation that had a lot of unknowns, after much discussion with my mother, we decided to look into it. We began talking to friends who had attended DeMatha or who had kids that had gone there. They all spoke highly of the school, mentioning its tradition of having a tight-knit community of students, the number of football players who had gone on to play in college and even the pros, and the excellent teachers and coaches. Of course, I realized they would be getting the quarterback that had beaten them, but I also felt that they were sincere. They all loved DeMatha.

Switching schools would be tough, since most of my friends were at Good Counsel. Once again, I would be leaving a comfort zone for a chance to play college football, and DeMatha, which had been a football powerhouse for decades, would provide that. Of course, my mother and Uncle Joe were in full agreement with my decision to have a day visit at DeMatha.

I was set up with a DeMatha sophomore to take me around classes and activities. Brendan Looney was a tough and talented safety and receiver and had played football on the varsity team as a sophomore, just as I had. Brendan would go on to attend the United States Naval Academy and served as a Navy Seal in Afghanistan, where he would make the ultimate sacrifice for his country. Brendan was one of the finest people I have ever met, and it was an honor to have been his teammate and friend.

Bill McGregor, who was the head coach of the DeMatha team, knew exactly what he was doing when he made Brendan my guide. Brendan was the type of person with whom I immediately felt comfortable. He was a straight-talking, look-you-in-the-eye type of guy who gave the impression of someone who would always have your back. We hit it off right from the start, and when I came home, I told my mother I wanted to be a DeMatha Stag.

I made my commitment, and I was going to enroll at DeMatha after Christmas break. Wow, what had I just done? I was really doing this. What was I going to tell my teammates and friends at Good Counsel? How was I going to explain to them that I would be leaving our championship team to go play for a team that we had beaten earlier in the season?

I decided to keep this to myself at Good Counsel, but then in the locker room after gym class, Jamie Hart said he had heard a rumor that I was transferring to DeMatha. At first I denied it, but Jamie persisted and I admitted it, but I told him not to say anything until after Christmas break.

But Jamie let news of my transfer get out, and it spread like wildfire. By the time I went to the cafeteria for lunch, Kenny Gaskins, who was a senior and one of the team leaders, called me over to a table full of football players. "Rumor going around school is that you're transferring to DeMatha, Scott," he said.

I was sitting across the table from Kenny, who had a look that said, "Say it ain't so."

Every guy at the table was looking at me, their quarterback.

"Not true," I said in an unconvincing tone. I hated lying and wasn't any good at it.

"Yeah," Kenny said, looking around the table and then back at me. "Heard you spent a day walking around with one of their players."

I dropped my head, not wanting to look at my teammates. "Okay, I am transferring," I mumbled.

Kenny looked at me for a moment, his face so expressionless, it spoke volumes. "How, Scott," he said in a monotone voice, "can you leave for a team we just beat?"

Silence.

"Next season," Kenny said with a rise of aggravation in his voice, "your teammates were counting on you, and now you're going to leave them high and dry."

I felt like digging a hole and burying myself in it.

I was now known as a traitor and still had two weeks left at Good Counsel—two very uncomfortable weeks. The headmaster called me into his office and almost screamed at me for deserting the school. Then I had a meeting with my gym teacher, who told me that I was making the biggest mistake of my life.

My football coaches were upset, and after a couple of meetings with them, I felt as though I was the biggest traitor in the history of the school. At this point, the whole school knew, and I was considered an outcast, a turncoat. Kids I thought were my friends ignored me in the hallways between classes. Some of my teammates, though still speaking to me, were short and brusque with me. Jamie Hart and Brian Daly were my staunchest supporters during this difficult time; they ate lunch with me, hung out with me after school, and let one and all know they had my back.

Parents of players called my mother, asking, "Why would you do this? You are putting him in a school where he may sit on the bench." And then there were the crank phone calls, calling me every name in the book for leaving Good Counsel. I began to second-guess my decision and considered telling DeMatha I wasn't coming.

But I stayed the course, and when I walked out of my last midterm exam, I didn't look back. In a way, my classmates' treatment of me made it an easier decision. I was now a DeMatha Stag. My transfer even led to an article in the *Washington Post*. The article ended by mentioning that the last two starting quarterbacks at DeMatha had received athletic scholarships to college: *Bobby Weaver is at East Carolina and Sean Gustus has committed to Richmond.*

CHAPTER 3

DEMATHA

DeMatha is an all-boys Catholic school located in Hyattsville, Maryland, not far from the University of Maryland campus. The school first made a national name for itself back in January 1965 at a sold-out Cole Field House at the University of Maryland, when the basketball team, coached by the great Morgan Wooten, upset Power Memorial from New York City and their seven-feet-one phenomenon Lew Alcindor, who later became Kareem Abdul-Jabbar. DeMatha was and still is a place steeped in athletic tradition.

The first day of school was a day full of anxiety for me. DeMatha was smaller in size and population than Good Counsel. The shirt and tie weren't anything new, but the underclassman navy-blue blazer with the DeMatha Catholic school patch on the left pocket was.

I had enrolled in the middle of the school year, which meant new teachers, new classmates, and of course, new teammates. And the biggest change—no girls. I had a schedule card to follow, and over the course of the day I shared algebra class with Brendan Looney. That made things a little better, but I was beginning to wonder if I had made a huge mistake. The entire day was a stressful blur, and I already missed Good Counsel.

After classes, the football team had winter workouts under the supervision of the strength and conditioning coach, Ed King, who divided us up in shifts: sprints in the hallways, then chugging up and down staircases, and finally weight lifting in a small room off the gym, where the basketball team was practicing. It was like an indoor boot camp. I couldn't believe it. This was way more than at Good Counsel, where in the off-season we had weight lifting three times a week and that was it.

The entire experience seemed like a very hard job. I didn't get home until six thirty, and I had to eat dinner, do homework, and then do it all over again the next day.

Also that first day, I had been asked to play basketball for the DeMatha JV, but the team was already halfway through the season. Not sure I even wanted to stay at DeMatha, I said I was focusing on football and declined the offer.

But I was a big basketball fan, and DeMatha was ranked nationally with future college stars like Joe Forte, who would later become a Tarheel beast at the University of North Carolina; Keith Bogans, who would later dominate at Kentucky; John Day-Owens, who went on to star at tight end for Notre Dame; and Brian Westbrook, who played and starred at running back for Villanova and later the Philadelphia Eagles. We're talking gifted athletes. It was fun to go to games and watch those guys ball.

As fate would have it, during my first week at DeMatha, the Stags had a big game at Good Counsel, which I attended with Brian Daly. The moment I walked into the gym, I could feel the tension. It felt as if every single person was looking at me with an evil stare. Halfway though the game, the Good Counsel student section started a chant aimed at the DeMatha student section. "Where's your banner?" Good Counsel had just won a championship football season, on the team I had quarterbacked.

The DeMatha student section had a rebuttal and started to chant back, "Where's your quarterback?" I was sitting courtside in the middle of this, trying to be as inconspicuous as possible as both student sections verbally battled each other for the remainder of the second half.

The entire process of a new school overwhelmed me. By the end of the first week at DeMatha, I wanted to leave. I hated everything about the place—from the outdated, tiny school to the long commute from Rockville to Hyattsville. Most of all, I missed Good Counsel, where I was a star on and off the field. At DeMatha, I was just a new guy who would have to prove himself.

Complicating the process was the fact that my mother had purchased a new three-story townhouse in Rockville. My mother, Katie, and I had watched the entire process develop from the ground breaking to the finished product, taking the fifteen minute ride over every weekend to check on the progress. Our new home was beautiful, and I was looking forward to living in it.

The Saturday morning after my first week at DeMatha, we had packed up the last of our belongings from my grandmother's house. Grandma stood in the driveway, waving. A big smile split that indomitable expression of hers, but in her eyes was a glimmer of disappointment at losing us. For the nine years we had lived with my grandmother, she had chauffeured Katie and me to school events and athletic practices, never once giving the impression of it being a chore. Instead she viewed it more as an opportunity to spend time with her grandchildren. She was an amazing and generous woman who helped sew and patch back together the severed lives of her daughter and her two children with an abundance of love and care.

As we drove away, I thought of all the childhood memories in my grandmother's house, mine and Katie's. By the time I was eleven and Katie seven, my grandmother had slowed down and Katie had taken her place in sporting activities inside and outside the house.

Katie pitched me the Wiffle ball, which I'd smack time and again. She would chase after it and throw me another and another ... She never tired of it and never turned me down when I asked her to join me. And when I was having trouble with my control, pitching in Little League, I drew a chalk outline of a catcher's mitt on the side of the house, and Katie stood in a mock hitter's stance as I wound up into my pitching motion and threw a tennis ball against the house. We did this every day after school for a week until I regained my control.

In the autumn and early winter, Katie retrieved endless jump shots and fed them back to me. And there was one drill I could have never done with my grandmother. During my second season at Maplewood Football, I missed a couple of tackles in practice, so I devised a tackling drill. Downstairs, I would give Katie a couple of yards head start from the laundry room and through the hallway, and if she made it to the couch in the den before I could get to her, she was safe. Oftentimes she didn't make it, and I tackled her around the waist, and down we went. Never once did she complain, and never once did she get hurt.

It had been a few years since Katie and I had done any of those activities, and moving to our new home seemed like a further indication of leaving my childhood behind and stepping into a transitional stage before adulthood.

The first evening in our new townhouse, I was helping my mother unpack boxes stacked in the living room. "Mom," I said with a little catch in my voice, "I think I want to go back to Good Counsel."

She put down a set of folded sheets and sat on our new sofa, rubbing her eyes with the heels of her hands. "I'm too tired to deal with this," she said in a disgusted tone. She went into the kitchen and dialed a number. "Joe, Kathy McBrien. Can you come over tomorrow and talk some sense into my son?"

Sunday morning, after we returned from Mass at Holy Cross with my grandmother, Joe LaPietra was waiting in his car, parked across from our townhouse.

The two of us sat down at the dining room table. Joe told me in no uncertain terms that quitting DeMatha was not an option. If I wanted to play Division 1 college football, DeMatha *was* the right school for me. He also told me what he had told me before: "Scott, you can't quit every time things get rough in the beginning."

So I returned to DeMatha and soon fell into a tolerable rhythm. During winter workouts, I made friends with my teammates, who already respected me because I was known as the left-handed quarterback from Good Counsel that had beaten them earlier that football season. They knew I had some game.

Football at DeMatha was a different animal—structured and intense. I had never been around so many athletes in my life; it was as though I had just jumped from a high school to a college program.

The quarterback coach, Chris Baucia, was a former DeMatha player and Virginia Tech quarterback and punter, and he knew the game inside and out. On his route to school, Chris picked me up every morning at a parking lot on Rockville Pike where my mother dropped me off. He drove me to school and back home after practice, forty minutes each way. On the morning drive, we didn't talk much as he listened to Howard Stern's morning talk show on the radio.

On the ride home, we would talk more about our school day or football, but the best part of the ride was the actual drop-off. I had a Ping-Pong table in my garage, and every day after school we had a match. We were addicted to it and looked forward to it. Both of us were good at Ping-Pong, and some of the games were epic battles. Chris was a friend and coach who I looked up to for guidance and advice on things, much like Joe LaPietra at Maplewood.

As I got somewhat more comfortable at DeMatha, I considered playing on the golf team like I had done my freshman year at Good Counsel. I went to tryouts with my buddy Sam Weaver, who was a solid stick and played on the team, and I made it. Coach McGregor got wind of it and told me I needed to concentrate on football from here on in. I was now eating, breathing, and living football, but still, I was not sold on DeMatha.

Every time I saw any of my buddies on the Good Counsel football team at a party or a dance, they would tell me to come back. "We need you, Scott," Brian Daly told me more than once. It weighed on me to hear my best friend almost pleading with me to come back. "It's where you belong."

When the school year ended, I told my mother I wanted to return to Good Counsel. DeMatha was too far, and the facilities were old and outdated, but most of all I missed my friends and the familiarity of Good Counsel.

We were eating dinner at the dining room table, and my mother put down her knife and fork and looked at me like, *You have got to be kidding me.*

"Come on, Scott," she said in a steady voice. "Remember why you decided to transfer?" She lifted her brow. *Well?*

"Why can't you ever make your mind up, Scott?" Katie said from across the table.

Katie had been living through the various ordeals of her older brother changing his mind since I first joined and then quit the flag football team Brian Daly had talked me into joining.

I turned my attention to my mother. "I know," I said, "but—"

My mother interjected, "Great coaches, great team, great tradition." She raised a finger as if to indicate one more thing. "And the opportunity to have scouts from Division 1 programs watch you play and provide you an athletic scholarship to their school." She raised her hands, palms up. "That's what you want, isn't it, Scott—to get a scholarship and play in college?"

Of course I knew she was right, but what finally got me over the hump was the skill with which players at DeMatha—quarterbacks, receivers, and running backs—played in seven-on-seven football in a summer league at local parks in Prince George's County. It was passing only, no running plays. Just me throwing the ball. It was no contact and a chance for me to learn our passing game and work on timing and execution with my receivers. It was organized backyard football, and it was a blast. The quarterback had five seconds to throw without a rush.

We were loaded with talent: Danny McNair, Jamal Jones, Dennard Wilson, Kenny Dantzler, Marvin Brown—who switched to fullback from tackle—Brendan Looney, John Day Owens, and Cameron Wake. Every one of them went on to play Division 1 football. Wilson, Owens, and Wake were drafted into the NFL.

We played other high schools in the area, and we also participated in weekend tournaments. Seven-on-seven was not fair for the defense, since they had to cover downfield for at least five seconds, but it was great work for both sides of the ball. By the end of summer league, I had formed a bond with my teammates and was all in and committed to DeMatha.

In August, the entire DeMatha team reported for summer camp. We didn't have a football field—our home games were played at Parkdale High in Riverdale, Maryland—so we practiced at Riverdale Park on a bare-bones, raggedy field. My teammates and I got dressed in the parking lot. That's right, the parking lot. Eighty guys getting down to their skivvies and strapping on their pads and practice uniforms.

The camp was brutal two-a-days that were physically demanding and mentally taxing, but I learned a lot of football, and by the end of camp I had won the starting job at quarterback.

Chris Baucia taught me how to read a defensive coverage. Where were the safeties? How many were deep? What was the depth of the corners? If there was one single high safety deep in the middle of the field and the corners were off ten to twelve yards, it was most likely going to be Cover 3, and I knew I could throw hitches and fades on the outsides all day. If there were two safeties deep on the hash marks and the corners were about five to seven yards off, I had a pretty good idea that they were going to be in Cover 2, and I knew that hitches and fade routes on the outsides were now taken away.

At Good Counsel, I hadn't had to know any of that. I called the play in the huddle and ran it no matter what the look of the defense was. At DeMatha, I had to read defenses and make checks at the line of scrimmage based on how the defense was aligned. This skill set would become a great asset for me in college.

And then there was the head coach, Bill McGregor, one of the best high school football coaches in the country. The assistant coaches on his staff were top-flight as well. DeMatha was where I learned the game of football. The offense was so much more complex and detailed than anything I had previously experienced. I was taught how to read defensive fronts and secondary coverages. I had the freedom to check out of plays and audible according to the defensive look. It was a whole new ball game for me, coming from Good Counsel.

DeMatha was a football program that prepared kids for the collegiate level. That was, and still is, why college coaches are a constant presence at the school. It was clear to me now: this was the reason I had transferred. Back then there was no social media, recruiting sites, or ways to promote yourself. Bill McGregor was a well-known and respected coach, and I knew that if I played for him, I was going to get looks from college coaches.

Once school began, we returned to practicing after school. This was my junior year of 1997, and besides the excellent skill players, we had a dominant offensive line, so I didn't have to throw the ball much. My first game, which we won handily, I completed two out of four passes, one for a touchdown, against Wilson High School. There was little need to pass with our powerful running game.

As the season went on, I was allowed to throw more often, but still the running game was our strength. But we were winning, and I was fine with it.

The big game I had circled on the schedule was our eighth game of the season against my old teammates from Good Counsel. We *could not* lose this game. I had to prove to myself that transferring had been the right move. I was nervous and treated it as the biggest game in my football career. Good Counsel was good but not as good as the championship team I had played on the year before, and they did not appear on paper to be at the same level as my undefeated DeMatha team. But I was taking nothing for granted.

We ended up crushing them 38–0, which was a huge relief for me. After the game, I shook hands with the Good Counsel players and coaches, but I could see in the coaches' eyes that they were still upset with me for leaving Good Counsel. Most of the Good Counsel players seemed to have moved on.

We finished the season undefeated and faced Gonzaga in the WCAC championship game at Byrd Stadium in a torrential downpour.

Gonzaga had an excellent head coach in Maus Collins, who was one of the most respected coaches in the DC area. Maus always found a way to get the best out of his players each and every year.

In the opening drive, we took the ball right down the field, and I ended up scoring from one yard out on a QB sneak to go up 7–0. That was the first and last time we would score all game, which was full of turnovers and slop. Nobody on either offense played particularly well, but Gonzaga made fewer mistakes, and we ended up losing 14–7 in a driving rain that lasted all four quarters. I was devastated. All that hard work and a perfect season down the drain.

We returned to off-season training, followed once again by seven-on-seven in the summer, but with Chris Baucia implementing a new aerial attack. "Scotty," he told me the first day, "we're gonna open it up this upcoming year."

For DeMatha, this was a complete change of strategy. It had always been a run first attack. Longer pass patterns were introduced into the offense, and we demolished teams. We were unstoppable, winning all of our seven-on-seven games. We even won multiple weekend tournaments that we traveled to over the course of the summer. I could hardly wait for the season to start.

But first we had to go through the grueling two-a-days, which part of me dreaded but another stronger part accepted, because my senior year, the Stags were ranked number two in the *Washington Post* behind quarterback Chris Kelley's powerhouse Seneca Valley squad in Germantown. College scouts would be attending our games in droves.

My teammates and I still had a sour taste in our mouths from the previous year, and we were determined to get back to that championship game and win the WCAC title. Besides our outstanding group of receivers, DeMatha had a strong offensive line, and I was now considered a savvy vet at the quarterback position.

We aired it out an average of fourteen times a game, the first time the Stags had expanded its passing attack since the great Tim Strachan quarterbacked the team.

Our aerial attack was hard to stop. The patterns themselves were nothing out of the ordinary, but my receivers were so fast and talented that we were running like a well-oiled machine. I had a big season and ended with twenty-five touchdown passes and zero interceptions.

One game that stood out during this season was at Gonzaga. We were out for revenge after they beat us the year before in the title game. To help motivate our teammates, Brendan Looney told me that he wanted to hang a Gonzaga jersey on the practice field goalpost earlier in the week leading up to the game.

After our last class, we hustled over to the field before anyone arrived. Brendan told me to drive underneath the goalpost, and he scrambled up on the top of the car and taped the jersey on the crossbar.

I parked the car in the parking lot, and we put on our practice gear. Our teammates showed up and saw the jersey.

"Where did that come from?"

"What!"

Then the coaches showed, and none of them said a word about the jersey until after practice. Coach McGregor gathered the team around and pointed to the jersey. "Simply put," he said, "that is who we need to beat."

Gonzaga was our archrival, and the entire school was revved up. During the week, the vibration of anticipation from the student body seemed to grow a little more pronounced each day in the hallways between classes.

Friday before practice, we found a message on the team bulletin board:

Game 5 DeMatha vs. Gonzaga October 3, 1998
A man can be as great as he wants to be. If you believe in yourself and have the courage, the determination, the dedication, the competitive drive and if you are willing to sacrifice the little things in life and pay the price for the things that are worthwhile. It can be done.

Once a man has made a commitment to a way of life, he has put the greatest strength in the world behind him. It's something we call heart power. Once a man has made this commitment, nothing will stop him short of success.

Teams that win are physical and play together. DeMatha is tough on you—to make you special.

Some might consider this over-the-top or hokey, but to me it was little things like this that made playing and attending DeMatha a special experience in my life.

Whether this helped inspire the team is hard to say, but I did have my best game as a DeMatha Stag. The game was sold out, and people were standing on the sidewalk off North Capital Street, watching through the fence at Buchanan Field.

Playing our archrival before a full house, I started off by throwing a forty-yard touchdown pass to my go-to target, Jamal Jones, on a deep post. What a feeling to be quarterbacking behind a powerhouse line with an abundance of talented skill players to pick from. I went eight for eight before my first incompletion. But Gonzaga had talent as well, and it was a hard fought, take-no-prisoners battle from the get-go. We ended up winning 26–13, and I finished the game with three touchdown passes.

After completing the season without a loss, there remained only one obstacle left—facing Gonzaga in the WCAC title game at Robert F. Kennedy Stadium in Washington, DC.

Gonzaga had some quality players such as Curome Cox, a defensive back who would go on to play with me at Maryland, and their do-everything player J. D. Schmidt, who played quarterback and linebacker.

Gonzaga couldn't stop our passing attack in the win during the season, and Coach McGregor figured Maus Collin would make adjustments. So we ran the ball and ran the ball. I only threw six passes in the game. Kenny Dantzler, a top-notch tailback, had a huge game, running for more than three hundred yards, and we won 49–13 to finish the season as the first team in DeMatha history to go 12–0. We ended up ranked thirteenth in the country by *USA Today*.

The season had been a grind, and I was worn out from getting up early every morning and driving myself to Hyattsville, attending classes, driving to practice, driving home, eating dinner, and doing homework until lights out.

But there was no time to rest, for this was the beginning of a new season—college recruiting. I had received letters of interest since my junior year from college programs. But that was a long way from an offer to play. I was five feet eleven on a good day and 150 pounds—small for a Division 1 program. Most schools were looking for quarterbacks six feet two and taller with a cannon arm or super-quick reflexes combined with blazing speed to run an option offense. Though I had above average speed and quickness, my strengths were my decision-making skills and accuracy in throwing the ball down the field.

One recruiter that had shown a special interest in me was a young assistant coach from University of Maryland named Mike Locksley, who had played at Ballou High School in Washington, DC, and had been in touch with me since my junior year.

During the course of my senior season, Coach Locksley would sometimes call me at home to say hello, compliment me on a recent game, or ask about school. He was the type of person who seemed genuinely interested in me, and I sensed that he thought I was his type of player. This was more of a gut sense on my part, that this man saw something in me beyond my limited size. And I knew Coach McGregor was talking me up to him.

Finally, I was invited to Maryland for an official visit, though part of me wondered if it was because I played nearby at DeMatha and also as a favor to Coach McGregor, who every year had a ton of Division 1 talent on his roster. Either way, I was excited about it. An old teammate of mine from Maplewood, Kevin Brant—who had starred at Walter Johnson High in Bethesda—and I were dropped off at the Sheraton near the university on Friday night and checked into our rooms.

Shortly after, our chaperones—mine was Todd Wike, a redshirt freshman offensive lineman—picked us up and drove us to a local saloon-restaurant in College Park. I was having a blast, drinking beer and soaking in the college experience until Mike Sherman, a senior lineman for the Terps and a Good Counsel graduate, who knew all about me leaving his old school for DeMatha, came over to my table with a shot of whiskey and told me to drink up if I knew what was good for me.

I was never much of a drinker, and after three shots, the next thing I knew we were attending a party at a house that members of the girls' volleyball team rented. It was probably a great party, but I remember very little.

The next morning, I woke up in my hotel room with a splitting headache and gut-wrenching upset stomach. Kevin and I, along with other recruits, had to take a tour of the campus. I thought I was going to die. I made three stops at the men's room along the way and puked myself dry.

That night, all the recruits and their parents were invited to dinner at Head Coach Ron Vanderlinden's house. Still queasy and not wanting to embarrass myself and my mother, I skipped out on the dinner. My mother was not pleased. But I didn't want to regurgitate my food over the head coach's dinner table.

The next morning, each player and his parents were to meet in Coach Vanderlinden's office to find out if they would receive a formal offer to attend Maryland on a football scholarship.

My mother and I saw Coach Locksley outside the football complex, and he told me he was looking forward to coaching me next year. I was thrilled. I was going to be a Terp! All I had to do was go through the formality of meeting with Coach Vanderlinden and accept his offer.

But, like a lot of things in life, the meeting with the head coach didn't go as I expected. I was told that no offer was coming presently but that it was a possibly in the future. *What?* To this day, I still wonder if my not showing for the dinner had something to do with it.

After exiting the meeting with Coach Vanderlinden, my mother and I saw Coach Locksley, and I told him that Coach Vanderlinden had not offered me a scholarship. Mike was shocked; this was news to him. But his eyes lit up as if an idea had just come to him.

"I want you to walk on as a punter, Scott, and within a semester I guarantee you can win a scholarship as a quarterback," he said.

"Coach," my mother said, "that's fine, but if Scott gets an offer from another Division 1 school, we're taking it."

On the ride home, I sat in the passenger seat, shoulders slumped, staring off into space. Outside it was a chilly, overcast day, which fit both our moods perfectly.

"Don't worry, Scott," my mother said in an unconvincing voice. "Something will come along."

We came to a red light on New Hampshire Avenue. She glanced over at me and started to speak. Then the light changed green, and we drove the rest of the way home in silence.

I did have another card to play. Rhode Island had offered me an official visit. Floyd Keith was the head coach, and he wanted me badly. The Rams, a Division 1AA school, were a couple of notches down in the collegiate pecking order from Maryland, but with no other offers, I decided to take them up on the visit.

After the great season I had at DeMatha, it felt good to be wanted. My mother and I flew up one cold, damp weekend in January, and during my Sunday exit meeting, Coach Keith offered me a full ride—my entire education for free. He told me I was the type of quarterback he wanted and gave me a strong sales pitch on Rhode Island.

I didn't commit right away, deciding to wait on a Division 1 offer. But it felt reassuring to have a scholarship offer in my pocket to fall back on.

Less than two weeks before the February signing day when players had to make their commitments, Dan Simrell, the quarterback coach from West Virginia University, called my mother at the house and said he was visiting recruits in the area and wanted to stop by tomorrow and visit with me. My mother called my Uncle Joe and asked him to be there for support.

Next day at five o'clock, Dan Simrell arrived and went to the basement with me and Uncle Joe to look at DeMatha games on tape. As we watched the game film, Coach Simrell asked me questions about formations and play calls, all of which I answered without hesitation. "Against the Cover 3, with a single high safety, I am looking for a fade."

I could tell he was impressed, not only with my play on the field but also with my knowledge of reading a defense.

Coach Simrell ended up having a beer with Uncle Joe and staying for dinner. He told us he would like to take a couple of my DeMatha tapes back to West Virginia and show them to the head coach, Don Nehlen.

Dan Simrell called the following day and told my mother that Coach Nehlen would like us to come up the next weekend for an official visit.

On the following Friday afternoon, my mother and I made the three-hour drive from Rockville to Morgantown. I didn't know a lot about the school, but I was impressed with the setting, architecture, and infrastructure of the main campus. Situated along the banks of the Monongahela River, with the mountains in the background, the downtown campus was dominated by stately redbrick buildings adorned with shingled mansard roofs, cupolas, and towers. A rapid transit shuttle called the PRT (personal rapid transit)—it was the only one in the country for a college, as I later learned on a tour—ran along the river and connected the three school campuses.

I was assigned a host, Tim Love, a defensive lineman from Ohio, and I also met my future roommate, Brian King, who was a defensive back from Damascus, Maryland. That evening, five or six other recruits and I had dinner at a restaurant with the coaching staff. Afterward, our hosts took us on a tour of downtown Morgantown. Everything was low-key. I did not want a repeat of my performance at Maryland!

On Saturday morning, all the recruits toured the football facilities, which were comprised of two outdoor fields, an indoor field, and an impressive athletic complex with an indoor track, a training room with whirlpools and rehab tubs, and a huge weight room. What a difference from the crammed spaces at DeMatha.

Upon entering the football complex, our eyes were drawn to navy-blue jerseys with gold numerals and lettering hanging on the walls, with our names and high school numbers on the back. We were duly impressed.

The first player I met in the weight room was Jerry Porter from Coolidge High School in Washington, DC. Jerry was already a big star who played multiple skill positions, including quarterback in a pinch. He asked me where I was from. I told him DeMatha, and I will never forget the expression on his face: *whaaat?* After we chatted a bit about DC area high school sports, he told me he hoped I would become a Mountaineer. At this point I was all in, except I hadn't been offered a scholarship yet. After touring the football complex, we saw the stadium. The sun was high and strong in the sky, reigning over the sixty-five-thousand-seat structure. One of the messages on the jumbotron read: *"Welcome, #8, Scott McBrien.* That was a wow moment for me. I wanted to be a part of this program so badly.

On Sunday morning, my mother called the football office and asked if she was to go with me to meet with Coach Nehlen, who had been a head coach at Bowling Green and West Virginia for thirty years, for my scheduled meeting. She was told that he definitely wanted her to come.

We were ushered into Coach Nehlen's office, and after introductions, he turned his attention to my mother and said, "Do you know why I wanted to meet you, Kathy?"

My mother shrugged and said, "I suppose to see what type of family Scott is from."

"No," Coach Nehlen said with a shake of the head. "I wanted to see how tall you are." He lifted his brow to see if we were getting his drift. "Because I believe players inherit their height from the mother's gene pool, and you sure have some height." My mother was five feet nine.

He offered us seats facing his desk and said, "Can I get you folks anything to drink?"

We declined.

Coach Nehlen leaned forward in his chair, hands folded on his desk. He gave the impression of a gentleman through and through, someone you could trust, an older, solid-as-a rock sort of man. He seemed as though he was glad to be in our company and had all the time in the world, not the buzz saw energy of most football coaches.

By this point, I was dying to know one thing and one thing only: *Coach, are you giving me a scholarship?* But I sat there and waited, the tension pinging between my mother and me.

"And the facilities, Scott," Nehlen said with a lift of his brow. "How did you like them?"

"They're unbelievably great, Coach … Everything here is great."

Coach Nehlen nodded as if liking what he was hearing. "Scott, would you like to be a Mountaineer?"

I froze for a moment, trying to ascertain that I had heard correctly. I glanced at my mother with a look that said, *Is this really happening?*

"I absolutely want to be a Mountaineer, Coach."

The ride home was like floating on a cloud for my mother and me. I called Uncle Joe and Joe La Pietra and told them the good news. My mother and I laughed and recalled the entire visit, especially the meeting with Coach Nehlen.

"Mom," I said through an ear-to-ear grin, "I thought I was going to explode when he offered me the scholarship."

My mother hooted a laugh and said, "Me too, honey. Me too."

We were thrilled. She loved that the school was only three hours away and that I was in the hands of someone the quality of Don Nehlen.

A week later, I mailed my acceptance paperwork to West Virginia, and for the first time in high school, I had no obligations toward football other than working out on my own. It was great. I was like a regular student. It was a lot of little things, like joining a recreation basketball team and playing hoops in the evening, going to the mall or out with classmates after school and getting something to eat. The pressure was off. I had earned a scholarship to a Division 1 program.

West Virginia had mailed me a workout plan with various exercises to perform, so I would either go to the DeMatha weight room with other seniors who had earned scholarships or join some of my Good Counsel friends like Josh Ott and Jamie Hart at the weight room at Georgetown Prep.

That summer was a blast, working out with my buddies who had also gotten football scholarships. I also spent two weeks at Bethany Beach. Life was good. But as soon as I returned home from the beach, I had less than a week before I had to report to training camp, and an old acquaintance returned to the pit of my stomach. *Pressure.*

MOUNTAINEER FOOTBALL

I was on edge the entire trip up to Morgantown. I was scared, excited, and anxious all at the same time. My mother, sensing this, tried to initiate conversation, but I mostly replied with a nod or an uh-huh. I felt as though I were closing a door, leaving my known world behind me and entering a world of unknowns.

Late in the afternoon, we pulled into a hotel near the WVU campus, which was going to be my home until the end of training camp. We unloaded my gear into the room, and then Brian King and his parents arrived. It was great to see a familiar face.

After Brian unloaded, we all got in the Kings' SUV and drove to a grocery store and stocked up on snacks and Gatorade.

In the hotel lobby, we met some other players and their parents. It was good to see other faces that had the same look of apprehension I was feeling.

The players had a team meal to report to, so I walked my mother out to the car. I was afraid that if I looked at her for too long, I would break out crying.

Kathy McBrien wrapped her arms around me, her only son and oldest child.

"Remember, Scott," she said through an I-love-you smile, "I'm just a phone call away."

She later told me that she cried the entire three-hour ride back to Rockville.

After dinner with the other incoming freshmen, we reported to a meeting at the hotel, where Don Nehlen addressed us. He spoke in a calming, steady-as-you-go voice, giving us a rundown of the schedule for the upcoming camp. (Freshmen reported a week early.) His demeanor was energetic but with a sort of vigorous kindness that allowed me to calm down. I felt as though my new teammates and I were in good hands.

The next morning was a shock for Brian and me when the coaches banged on our door at five-thirty and then opened it. (They had keys to all the rooms.)

"Get up. Breakfast in ten minutes," a demanding voice barked.

My first thought was that many of my friends were still at the beach and I was preparing to go through football boot camp. It was moments like this when I hated football, knowing what I was about to endure. But I had a family and relatives and friends who were invested in my football journey, and quitting would have let them all down. Sometimes I thought I was doing it as much for them as for myself.

On the first day of freshman camp, there was another quarterback, a stud from Flint, Michigan. He was six feet four, 220 pounds, fast, and oozing with athleticism. He looked every bit like the four-star recruit he had been designated. But I had been fighting an uphill battle since the get-go, and I said to myself, "Bring it on."

The camp was structured and regimented, much like at DeMatha, as we moved from drill to drill, signaled by blaring horns. It didn't take long before I realized I was the better quarterback. My accuracy was better, my footwork was better, and I had received a better football education at DeMatha. Thank you, Bill McGregor and Chris Baucia. I now realized that I could compete at this level. One practice and I knew.

Don Nehlen ran a pro-style offense. The only difference from DeMatha was that Coach Nehlen used the shotgun formation from time to time in passing situations. At WVU, the terminology and some of the schemes were a little different, but it wasn't any more complicated than DeMatha.

The following week the upperclassman reported. The linemen were easy to pick out. I had played with some big guys in high school, but all of these Mountaineer linemen were enormous. I had never been around so many large human beings in my life. The upperclassman had to go through a conditioning test, and after our afternoon practice, we got to watch them go through it.

Some of the players had completed their tests earlier in the week and joined us in the bleachers. One behemoth sat next to me and introduced himself. John Conte told me to lean on him if I had any questions about anything—practice, school, etc. I thanked him but had no clue who he was or what position he played, and I didn't think much more about it.

On the first day of practice, I was on the field with the quarterbacks, and our starter Marc Bulger took warm-up snaps with the starting center—John Conte, who it turned out was one of the leaders of the team.

During that first camp, John gave me pointers and tips, such as to when to call a check down on inside drills. "Run to the shade, Scott," he'd say, meaning run toward the side of the center where the nose tackle is lined up. Or he'd tell me when to try to get the defense to go offside. "They're jumpy, Scott, call the play on two."

On the depth chart below Bulger—who was a senior and a Heisman Trophy candidate and would go on to play eight years in the NFL, including two Pro Bowl appearances—were two sophomores and then me.

Once camp started, I had to take a backseat, and I spent a lot of time during practice standing on the sidelines. When my number was called to quarterback in a drill or scrimmage, I made the most of my limited time. Soon I got a chance to run the scout team, which was tasked with imitating our upcoming opponent's offense.

The coaches took notice of me hitting the receiver in stride, picking the defense apart, and running the offense like I knew what I was doing. In a way, I felt no pressure since I knew there was little chance of me playing anytime soon with three players ahead of me on the depth chart.

But as the camp progressed, I received more playing time in scrimmages and drills. On the last day of camp, I was promoted to third-string quarterback.

That evening, the entire team sat in the stadium under the lights as the school marching band played on the field, strutting their stuff. This was a tradition started by Coach Nehlen, and it was moving and awesome. To sit there in that great stadium, the field flooded in light, with the booming drums and horn instruments playing against each other ... To this day I get chills thinking about it.

While I sat there absorbing that emotional moment, I realized that not only was I in a top-flight Division 1 program but that I had advanced far in a short period of time as a quarterback. I began to wonder if I had a chance to play this year instead of redshirting, which allows a player to sit out one year and not lose eligibility. And I was gaining the respect of the upperclassmen, who realized I had some game to me. I was now known by some of my teammates as the Little Lefty.

After the band ceremony, the team had a final meeting, signifying the end of training camp. Brian and I checked into our dorm room in Bennett Tower, situated on Evansdale Campus, nearly two miles north of the Downtown Campus. The third campus was Health Sciences, where Mountaineer Field was located. Besides commuters, all freshmen at the school were required to live in a dorm for their first year, and we assimilated with the rest of our classmates.

By this time, Brian and I were inseparable. Having both grown up in Montgomery County, we came from similar backgrounds, were about the same size, and were comfortable in each other's company. We reported to and left practice together, ate all three meals together, took the PRT to the same classes, and attended study hall after dinner with the other freshman players. It got to the point that our teammates began kidding us that if they saw one of us, they knew the other was nearby.

Our first game was in Charlotte, North Carolina, at Ericsson Stadium, home to the Carolina Panthers. I was one of only two true freshmen—running back Quincy Wilson was the other—who traveled with the team to this game. This was a pretty big deal, and John Conte even picked me up at my dorm and drove me to the team bus.

We were playing East Carolina in a game titled the East-West Showdown, and the seventy-five-thousand-seat stadium was packed with plenty of Mountaineer fans. West Virginia, I was beginning to understand, had a rabid fan base that traveled to all away games in large numbers, arriving in anything from ratty pickups to huge pimped-out RVs. Before and after the game, I spoke briefly with Bobby

Weaver, who had been three years ahead of me at DeMatha and played H-back for East Carolina.

In the third quarter, with West Virginia leading, Marc Bulger sprained his knee, and the second-string quarterback, redshirt sophomore Brad Lewis, went in. If he got hurt, I was in! I was scared to death. At this point, I didn't feel ready to play in a game being played at a faster speed than I had ever seen before. Besides, I would lose a year of eligibility if I played.

Every time Brad went back to pass, I was greatly concerned that if he got hit hard and was taken out, I was in. I wanted to play, but I was nowhere near ready, and I didn't want to lose a year of eligibility for limited playing time. We ended up losing the game 30–23, but Brad made it through, and my redshirt was saved for the moment.

Our next game was the home opener, which we won against Miami of Ohio 43–27, but what I remember most about that day was the bus ride from our local hotel—a college football staple to keep players focused and away from distractions—to the stadium.

After a pregame meal and team meeting, three buses left Lakeview Golf and Resort for a twenty-minute ride to the stadium. A police escort led us onto Interstate 68 to the university exit, leading us past the bottled up traffic.

Fans were sticking their heads out of the windows of their vehicles, hooting and hollering and waving school flags at us. We entered the parking lot, which was packed with tailgaters who roared encouragement to us. These folks took Mountaineer football seriously, very seriously.

Though the team did not do well, finishing our season 4–7, I maintained redshirt eligibility, but it was not easy. Toward the end of the season, which was already lost, both Marc and Brad were out with injuries, and instead of putting me in, Coach Nehlen inserted Jerry Porter—who played receiver and defensive back, plus returned kicks—in at quarterback, thus saving me a year. A lot of coaches wouldn't have done that, but Coach Nehlen was looking after the long-term interest of the program and me.

At the end of the season, I felt as though I had made great leaps, not only as a player. I was in a happy place, as was Brian. We were part of a family that practiced together, studied together, and went to parties together, and on weekends the older guys would hit the bars in town together.

Though the season was over, I had my eye on the upcoming spring practice and an opportunity to be the starting quarterback in the fall.

5

PLAYING TIME

Spring ball was new to me, which was four weeks of practice, ending in the spring game. I had never played football in the springtime before, and it seemed strange at first, but I soon got into the rhythm of it, as there was a starting job I was competing for.

Brad Lewis had a strong spring. He was your prototypical Division 1 pro-style quarterback, six feet three, 220 pounds. By this time I was six feet tall, but only weighed 160 pounds. Physically there was no comparison, but I held my own during spring camp. I now had a good understanding of the offense and was confident in my ability if my number was called to play in a game.

The spring game, in which the team is divided up into two teams, was another shock for me. Twenty thousand people attended the game. A spring football game. This was by far the biggest crowd I had ever played in front of. I was nervous, but I executed and played a solid game with two touchdown passes.

Brad and I would enter fall camp competing to win the starting quarterback job, but I could tell Coach Nehlen was leaning toward Brad, who had been in the system two years longer, because he received more time with the first team during camp.

Still, I had come a long way in a short period of time, but first I had to get through a summer that, to this day, was the most physically demanding time of my life.

Most of the players spent the summer training on campus and taking summer school courses. During the season it was difficult to take a heavy load of schoolwork, with so much time devoted to football.

After the school year ended, Brian and I moved into an apartment off campus. This was our first time living on our own and our first taste of being independent. We had to open up a checking account to pay rent and utilities, cook our own meals, and keep the place clean.

Athletes who lived off campus were issued a stipend check of $600 each month. With that money, we were responsible for paying rent, utilities, and meals—if we wanted them outside the complex cafeteria—and the rest was spending money. Remember, this was West by God Virginia, and for a spacious two-bedroom, one bath apartment, our rent was $300 each. With our remaining money, we thought we were rich and couldn't wait for the check to hit our pockets each month.

With our own apartment, I figured over the summer it would be a nice break from the grind of the season. Was I ever wrong.

Al Johnson was the head strength trainer, and he worked our tails off. The weight training was beyond hard. It was grueling, set after set, from one weight station to the next. It was much longer and more strenuous than anything I'd experienced at DeMatha. After lifting, we went outside for exhausting conditioning drills that involved a lot of running. This went on for six long weeks.

At the end of the summer camp, Al decided on a conditioning test in which we had to run fifty 110-yard sprints. Lineman had to complete each one in sixteen seconds, linebackers fourteen seconds, and skill players twelve seconds. After each sprint, we had forty-five seconds to recover before doing it again.

It was so brutal that some of the players snuck off and hid in the stadium stairwell. Others puked their guts out between sets.

I thought I was going to die, and I was the lightest guy out there. By the time we reached the forty-second sprint, a member of the medical staff came out and told Al to end the session before he killed someone. After that, we referred to our strength and conditioning coach as Crazy Al Johnson.

After surviving summer camp, I spent two weeks at Bethany Beach—savoring every minute of it—and then reported to fall camp. Physically, the camp was a breeze compared to the summer, but now the pressure was back, as I was competing for the starting quarterback job.

Brad and I both played well in camp, but his experience in the system won out, and he got the nod. I was entrenched as the backup and knew I would get some playing time in either mop-up duty or if Brad got hurt.

Our first game was at home against Boston College. Some fans arrived in the parking lot in their RVs on Thursday before the Saturday game. By the time our team bus arrived at the stadium, they were going absolutely nuts. Redneck hillbillies in overalls, with long beards and tattoos, looked like they had recently migrated from the backwoods, down off the mountain, and into the parking lot at Mountaineer Stadium.

Before kickoff, the stadium was full, and in a loud, frenzied state, half the stadium was screaming, "Lets gooooooo!" and the other half was responding, "Mountaineeeeeerrssss!" It was so loud it seemed like the stadium might implode. Talk about a home field advantage. We won the game 34–14, and I received my first collegiate snap from center—a moment I will never forget—when I got mop-up duty in the fourth quarter.

As I came to the line of scrimmage, I saw my good friend from Good Counsel, Josh Ott, on the other side of the ball at middle linebacker. It was weird because every time I called a play, I had to point out the middle linebacker to set the line protection and blocking scheme—in this case, Josh. After the game, we chatted briefly and then returned to our own football universes.

After six games our record was 4–2, with losses to two top-notch teams: the Miami Hurricanes and Virginia Tech Hokies. At this point, I had yet to see significant playing time.

Our next game was at home with Notre Dame coming to Morgantown for a three-thirty game that would be broadcast nationally on NBC. During the week leading up to the game, the excitement grew each day, not only among the players but also on campus and in town. The Fighting Irish were coming! Worlds were colliding.

By kickoff, there were more than sixty-five thousand fans in attendance, with nary an empty seat in the house. The stadium was a madhouse, a constant roar of mostly Mountaineer fans but also of a respectable number of Irish fans packed in a corner of the end zone.

Late in the first quarter, Brad was sacked and came out of the game limping. Next thing I knew, I was in the huddle, calling a play with a 14–7 lead. I was nervous, out of whack, and I found it hard to focus. It came upon me so quickly. I was playing against Notre Dame in front of a full house and on national TV.

On my first play at the line of scrimmage, I thought my heart would burst out of my chest. The Notre Dame linemen, in their white uniforms and gold helmets, were like a mountainous wall of humanity. They were big boys. One shouted at me, "Fresh meat." Two linebackers came up toward the line, their eyes honed on me, reminding me of lions hunting for prey. I knew I should audible out to a quick pass in the flat, but my mind and body were not working together and the run play went nowhere.

I went three and out, three and out, interception, and three and out. Going into the locker room at the half, we were down 28–14, and I realized this game was at a different level from anything I had experienced. I also realized that I had not prepared enough for a game of this magnitude. I hadn't looked at enough film to understand the defense's tendencies in certain situations.

In the second half, the offensive coordinator Bill Legg began calling quarterback play action and bootlegs—playing to my strengths—and I soon settled down. But it was too little too late, as we lost 42–28. I racked up a lot of yardage, finishing with 252 passing yards and a touchdown pass.

In the locker room after the game, I felt awful, as if it were my fault that we lost. The seniors were upset, throwing gear against the walls, with tears in their eyes. It was their last chance to play in a big game on national television, and I felt as though I hadn't upheld my end of the stick to help them go out on top.

Khori Ivy, a starting receiver, was sitting at his locker, still dressed in his pads, with his head down, almost in tears. He'd wanted that one bad.

That loss changed the way I prepared as a quarterback during the week. I studied more on and off the field. I watched more film, studying defenses, defenses' tendencies, opponents' body language, and I took mental reps in practice when I wasn't getting physical reps. Any time I was not getting a rep, I would still act as if I was under center, read the defense, and mentally go through my reads and progressions. The loss to Notre Dame changed me as a quarterback. I began doing all the little things that I had not done before.

The following week, with Brad still out injured, I got my first start against Syracuse in Morgantown. I felt more prepared, having studied the game plan, which was to establish the running game and then mix in some passes as the game progressed. As I set up behind center on the first play from scrimmage, the middle linebacker pointed at me and said in a tone of gleeful vengeance, "Hey, son, the little league is down the street."

The "little league" game turned out to be a close one in which I played okay and made some clutch passes on third down, but my completion percentage was low, eight for twenty-one for 156 yards, with a couple of dropped passes. But we had the lead with around three minutes left and were driving down the field when a pass play was called—we were already in field goal range—and I threw an interception.

Syracuse drove down the field and scored a touchdown, resulting in West Virginia losing 31–27.

I headed toward our locker room, my head down, shoulders slumped. I was devastated. I felt an arm around my shoulder and knew immediately to whom it belonged. "Don't put your head down, Lefty," Coach Nehlen said to me.

I lifted my head and looked at my head coach.

"I'm proud of the way you hung in there today, Scotty," Coach Nehlen said with a tap on my shoulder before he veered off.

There's a saying that a man's true character is revealed in defeat. But what really made Coach Nehlen's act of kindness toward me even more unique was that in the locker room after the game, he told the team that he would be retiring at the end of the season. He had all that on his mind and had still taken the time to console me.

Don Nehlen was a grandfather figure to many of us, a good man who cared about each and every one of us. Some players were full-out crying in the locker room. This was a man who was in charge of a major part of our lives—football—and we were now facing the unknown. We were still kids, many in the bodies of grown men, and it felt as though we were about to lose a very important family member.

But we still had a season to finish, and on Monday before practice, some of the team leaders held a meeting to emphasize the importance of Coach Nehlen getting to a bowl game and going out a winner.

By this point in the season, I was beginning to gain some recognition on campus as a player on the team. But when they met me, the students and fans were shocked that at six feet and 160 pounds I was actually a football player. But for a redshirt freshman, it appeared I had a promising future as a Mountaineer quarterback.

That supposition was only strengthened when my next game action came in the last game of the regular season, in a border state rivalry known as the Backyard Brawl. Pittsburg and West Virginia—both with 6–4 records—were evenly matched teams and huge rivals, two blue-collar states represented by their blue-collar teams. Making it even more special was the fact that we were playing in the final college game at Three Rivers Stadium.

During the week leading up to the game, a lot of chatter went back and forth between players of both teams. More than a few of my teammates had played with or against Pittsburgh players in high school. This was like two families fighting for bragging rights for the entire year.

Brad Lewis wasn't playing well, and we went down 38–9. I entered the game and drove the team down the field and finished it off when I zipped a seventeen-yard touchdown pass to Khori Ivy. Then Lance Frazier returned an interception for a touchdown. We then stopped them, and on our next drive I threw a perfect pass to Ivy, but he dropped the ball in the end zone—a backbreaker.

With forty-nine seconds left in the game, I threw a sixty-yard touchdown pass to Phil Braxton, but it was too little too late, and we lost by a score of 38–28. But I had played my best game so far in my career—257 yards for two touchdowns and no interceptions—and my confidence was only growing.

Despite our 6–5 record, West Virginia was invited to play Mississippi in the Music City Bowl in Nashville. The Mountaineers had lost their last eight bowl games, and the upperclassmen on the team were determined to have Coach Nehlen break the streak and go out a winner.

Brad Lewis led the team to a huge lead at halftime and ended up throwing for over three hundred yards and five touchdowns. With ten minutes left in the third quarter, we were leading 49–9.

At this point, I was warming up to enter the game when the Rebels benched their starting quarterback and brought in a redshirt freshman named Eli Manning. I never saw a snap as Eli kept driving his team down the field for touchdowns, though we still won 49–38. It was the beginning of a brilliant collegiate and NFL career for Eli.

But what I thought was the beginning of my career was about to hit a major roadblock as the new coach at West Virginia was about to shake things up.

6

RICH ROD

Before the Music Bowl, Rich Rodriguez was announced as the new head coach at West Virginia. I didn't know anything about him other than that he had been the offensive coordinator at Clemson and he used an up-tempo spread offense. I got my first look at him during practice for the week of the bowl game. He stood off to the side and silently observed practice. The first thing that struck me about him was how young he looked. He was born in West Virginia and had played defensive back for Coach Nehlen back in the mid-1980s. He was a tall, fit-looking man, with dark hair cut military short, but it was his eyes that drew my attention. They were a drill sergeant's eyes.

By this point of my collegiate career, I was in my groove at West Virginia. I loved the school, my teammates, and being a part of a university and community that adored its football team. Life was good.

After Christmas break, we had our first team meeting with Coach Rodriquez and his youthful staff. One exception was the quarterback coach, Bill Stewart, who was a holdover from the previous staff. Before Coach Rodriguez spoke, the coaching staff handed out T-shirts with *Spot the Ball* written on the front.

Coach Rodriguez held up a shirt and ran his finger across the lettering. "This means we are going to do everything *fast*." He gave us a knowing lift of the brow—*Are we clear?* "We want to get back up on the line of scrimmage to snap the ball as soon as the ref spots it. Fast." He looked his players over, those drill sergeant eyes burning with intensity. "And it all begins," he said with a raised finger, "in winter workouts."

My first impression was that maybe this is what we needed—new blood, younger, more energetic blood.

Soon after we began our winter workouts, the new coaching staff, like their head coach, gave off a different vibe—a hard-charger vibe of everything being done fast—as they pushed us through drills.

If a player wasn't hustling enough to a coach's satisfaction, he had to wear an orange jersey at the next workout and was designated as an "Orange Eater." This meant that you might as well be on the sidelines enjoying an orange. It also made those players stand out as slackers. Besides the stressful workouts, I had to learn a new and unfamiliar offense that was a no-huddle, shotgun formation in which the quarterback was signaled plays from the sidelines.

By the time spring ball arrived, I was still having trouble digesting the offense and was getting limited reps. Coach Rodriguez was not patient with me or any other player who was not performing up to his expectations. There was lots of screaming and kicking balls when a play wasn't done to his satisfaction. It was wild. I had been screamed at by coaches my entire career, but this seemed different, at another level. There was an edge to it that not only I but also many of my teammates found unsettling.

But it seemed to me that Coach Rodriguez was more tolerant and patient with Brad Lewis and redshirt freshman Rasheed Marshall, who were my main competition for playing time, when they made a mistake in practice or couldn't answer a question in team meetings.

In a quarterback install meeting—where new plays were added to the playbook—Coach Rodriguez stood in front of a whiteboard, marker in hand. "When we're in ram formation and we're running all hooks—who is your read, McBrien?" His tone was demanding, impatient as though he already knew I didn't know the answer.

"Uh, uh, I know the formation but am not sure—"

Coach Rodriguez cut in with a raised voice, an angry voice: "You gotta know this, McBrien!"

Coach Rodriguez ran all the quarterback meetings, so I was constantly in his presence, and he was constantly on me. Watching film, the berating continued: "That was a JV throw!" and "Where's your read, McBrien?" He said it all with such aggravation that I had trouble thinking straight. If he was trying to rattle me, he had succeeded.

It continued on the practice field. When I threw late to a receiver or misread the defense, I would hear it: "We just went over this in the meeting, McBrien! Get your ass out of there. Rasheed get in there."

It wasn't his words as much as his irate tone that made me so uncomfortable and unsure of myself. Combine that with his body language—punting a ball into the stands when I messed up or tossing his hat angrily to the ground—and the look of hostility in those drill sergeant eyes.

It got to the point that on my first mistake in practice, Coach Rodriguez would yank me out. I was in constant fear of getting pulled from a scrimmage while at the same time trying to learn and execute a new offense. I was beginning to hate being a member of the Mountaineer family, something that a few months ago had seemed inconceivable. All of a sudden my life was miserable.

I began to wonder if Coach Rodriguez was trying to run me off the program to open another scholarship for a quarterback with blazing speed and the running ability of a tailback that fit his spread offense. There was a rumor floating around the team that a former five-star quarterback from West Virginia who had signed a professional baseball contract a few years back was considering ditching baseball and coming to West Virginia to play football.

My fear appeared to be coming to fruition when Coach Stewart had a meeting with me and asked me to consider switching positions and possibly trying out for receiver or punting duties. My heart sank to my stomach. I felt ill as I kept telling Bill Stewart that I wanted to play quarterback. That was who I was: Scott McBrien, quarterback. Any other option was not something I wanted or would do.

Coach Stewart relented and said I could stay at quarterback but that I had to step up my game come fall camp. I knew everything Coach Stewart had told me had come down from the head coach. He had just been the messenger.

So I went through summer camp at West Virginia, doing summer school and all the hard-core training with the strength coaches, plus studying the playbook and trying to learn the offense, but I did it all with a sense of doom hanging over me. I felt as though I was no longer wanted. I decided to give it my best effort come fall camp, and if it wasn't good enough, then I would cross that bridge when I came to it. Where I would go or do next, I didn't even allow myself to consider.

Two weeks at Bethany Beach was a welcomed respite, but it went quickly. Before I knew it, I was back at school in training camp.

By the second day of camp, Rasheed Marshall, who had speed, agility, and power—perfect for the spread offense—was promoted over me. I was now the third-string quarterback.

Camp was miserable. Coach Rodriguez was on my case every time I made a mistake. I couldn't think straight much less perform to the best of my ability. As in spring ball, I was more focused on not messing up to keep Coach Rodriguez out of my face than making my reads. One wrong call in the huddle or one fumble off the snap and I was sent to the sidelines.

"Get out of there, McBrien! Rasheed, get in there." All of this was done in the presence of the entire team. It was humiliating.

In a morning practice during the second week of camp, I dropped back to spot a receiver, didn't find anyone open, and held the ball, dropping my head. Coach Rodriguez ran over to me and slapped the ball out of my hands, screaming full-throttle right in my face: "You need to tuck and run!" For some reason, that was the tipping point for me. At that moment I knew I was done with this coach and a school I thought I would never leave.

After practice, I took a shower, went directly to my car, and headed toward Rockville, Maryland, without notifying anyone. I was upset, and my mind was in a fog, except for one thing: I was never going to play football again for Rich Rodriguez.

On I-68, I called my mother and told her what had transpired. At first, she tried to talk me into returning to school, but as the conversation progressed, she sensed how upset I was.

"Scott, calm down. I can tell you're upset. How fast are you going?"

I checked the speedometer. "Ninety," I said as I eased my foot off the accelerator. I hadn't had a clue how fast I had been going.

"Please slow the car down, Scott," my mother said, "and get home safely."

While I was trying to get myself home, my mother called Bill Stewart to let him know what I was doing. Then my cell phone began ringing with Bill Stewart's name on the screen. I didn't answer. I was not changing my mind.

For the next couple of days, Bill Stewart called the house and talked with my mother. He continued to call my cell phone, but I didn't pick up. I liked Coach Stewart, but I was not changing my mind. In hindsight, I could have handled this situation much better.

I wasn't sure if I was going to play football again, but in case I did, I needed my release from West Virginia. My mother then did something that, to this day, I am glad she made me do. Since I hadn't told anyone about leaving school, and also out of respect for the program, she insisted that she and I drive to West Virginia to have a face-to-face meeting with Coach Rodriguez and ask for my release in person. "It's the right thing to do, Scott," she told me. I grudgingly, very grudgingly, agreed with her.

Back in Morgantown, we went to my apartment and retrieved all my clothing and gear. My roommates at the time, Grant Wiley and Quincy Wilson, weren't there, which in a way was good. It was hard enough without having to see my good friends and ex-roommates.

The meeting was in a big conference room in the athletic facility. On one side of the table sat Rich Rodriguez and Bill Stewart. My mother and I were on the other.

My mother thanked them for the opportunity to meet with them. At this point they were probably thinking I wanted to come back. "Gentlemen," my mother said, "Scott has something to tell you."

They both looked at me.

"I am not coming back to West Virginia, and I would like my release," I said.

Things then got a little chippy, with Coach Rodriguez telling me if I quit now, I would quit later in life and end up washing cars. He also told my mother and me that he wasn't giving me a release, which meant I would have to wait two complete seasons before being eligible to play again, basically ending my college career.

My mother called a family friend and attorney Brian Tansey, who put a call into the athletic director at West Virginia. She also called Don Nehlen to see if he would talk to Coach Rodriguez. I'm not sure what did it, but a couple of days later I received my release.

Family and friends at Washington DC Touchdown Club banquet

Trent Dilfer and I at Washington DC Touchdown Club banquet

My sophomore year at Good Counsel

DeMatha skill players and Coach Chris Baucia my senior year. From left to right, Danny McNair, Brendan Looney, Tony Okanlawon, Nick Boccagno, Scott McBrien, John Day Owens, and Jamal Jones

Mountaineer Stadium during my first collegiate start

Maryland at Florida State, September 6, 2003

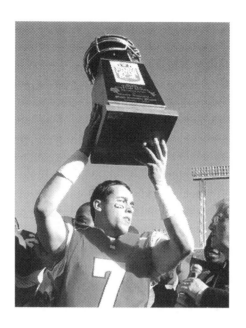

Gator Bowl MVP, January 1, 2004

West Virginia at Maryland, September 20, 2003

Maryland at Florida State, September 6, 2003

Scott McBrien with Steve Suter, James Franklin, and Matt Swope

CHAPTER 7

A NEW BEGINNING

Still unsure of whether to attempt to find a college program to play for, I met with my coaches from DeMatha, Bill McGregor and quarterback coach Chris Baucia.

"You proved last year that you can compete in Division 1," Chris said. We were in Coach McGregor's office. Bill sat behind his desk, with Chris sitting next to him while I sat facing them.

"Yeah," I said, "but I am just not sure I want to start all over."

"Why don't you come out to the afternoon practice and help Chris with the quarterbacks?" Bill said.

It was like old times, except I was on the sidelines instructing instead of being instructed. But the sights and sounds of all of it—the clap of shoulders pads colliding, the coaches shouting encouragement, the passing drills that I helped out on, and the lightning-quick receivers and defensive backs competing for passes—reinforced in me what I would be giving up if I quit playing.

After practice, Coach McGregor said he would put the word out that I was looking for a school to play at. He then suggested that I consider walking on at Maryland, which had hired a new head coach, Ralph Friedgen. Coach McGregor said their starting quarterback was a senior who would graduate by the time I was eligible to play. He also mentioned that I would be playing in front of family and friends. "It would be a good fit for you, Scott."

Bill then called Mike Locksley, who was coaching the running backs for the Terps.

Mike told Bill that if I walked on, he was confident that I would earn a scholarship by the end of the season. It meant the world to have a college coach say those words about me after what I had been through at West Virginia. The man had never wavered in his belief in me. Also, I was beginning to realize that I needed football in my life. I had not completed my journey and needed to see it through, not just for my family but for myself.

The next day, Coach Locksley called me and told me to report to campus. I only had two days to enroll in a college or lose a second year of eligibility. The day was a whirlwind as I was hooked up with the academic people, counseling, and administration.

After enrolling, I reported to my first meeting with Coach Friedgen, who was a Maryland alum. He had been a career assistant coach in college and the pros and was well respected in the coaching community as an offensive guru, especially in grooming quarterbacks. My first impression of him was that he was a big, gruff bear of a man who was all business. I sensed that he was a bit disappointed by my size. At this stage, I was barely 170 pounds and had reached my full height of six feet one. Not tiny but not big for Division 1 football.

Coach Friedgen began the conversation by asking me about my punting. I told him I was walking on as a quarterback. He told me fine but that he had five other quarterbacks on the roster and I would have to work my way up the ladder. He had little to lose with me trying out at quarterback since I wasn't on scholarship.

Ralph Friedgen was very busy at the time, and I imagined he had gotten a bit confused about who I was. Not an auspicious beginning to my career as a Maryland Terrapin.

Being a walk-on was much different from a scholarship player. My first semester I commuted to school and didn't eat with the team or attend study hall. I went to class, attended practice, and then drove home—a big comedown from playing against Notre Dame in front of sixty-five thousand fans in Morgantown just a short time ago.

I didn't even practice with the offense but with the freshmen and other walk-ons at the far end of the field, running the scout team. It was like purgatory. The only time I got noticed was when I ran the next opponent's offense against our defense. I had a field day picking the defense apart and was honored on multiple occasions as scout team player of the week.

Also, encouraging me was Mike Locksley, who didn't see me play, since he was upfield working with the offense, but he told me he was hearing great things about me. Little things like that gave me the impetus to keep at it. I hated the fact that after practice I had to drive home. I did not feel like a complete member of the team, but rather a part-timer.

But on Tuesday, September 11, 2001, football took a backseat when classes were suddenly canceled. I walked over to the student lounge of a teammate's dorm, only knowing that an airplane had collided with one of the Twin Towers in the World Trade Center in New York City. In the student lounge, I watched in horror as our country came under attack. A plane had crashed into the Pentagon, less than twenty miles from the Maryland campus.

At practice that day, Coach Friedgen held a team meeting and told the team that the upcoming home game against West Virginia might be canceled but that we would practice as if we would play. On Thursday, Coach told us that not only our game but all NCAA football games had been canceled for the week.

That was a sobering and thought-provoking week for me and my teammates. But we still had a season to complete, and football, for me, was a welcome respite from world events.

The following Monday, we went back to our regular practice routine. Maryland was loaded with talent, and by the fourth week of the season, the Terps were 3–0. Running back Bruce Perry and linebacker E. J. Henderson were major impact players who would both go on to play in the NFL, as would the starting quarterback, Shaun Hill. Our next game was the make-up game at home against none other than my old team, West Virginia. I knew every one of their signals, every play, every formation on defense and offense. Oh yeah!

That week of practice, Coach Friedgen had me in the defensive meetings, which I basically ran. I told the players as we watched film that if player X did this, they should expect that. If they lined up in this formation, we should expect this play. For example, I would say to our cornerbacks Curome Cox and Tony Okanlawon, "If they line up in a double-right formation, they like to run hitches and slants on the outsides." I could tell what plays they were going to run by the way they lined up. By the end of that week, Maryland's defense was ready and prepared.

Come game day, I was standing on the sidelines next to Coach Friedgen, calling out plays to our defense. If I saw a receiver in motion in a certain formation, I yelled out to Tony Okanlawon what to expect. "Slant left, Tony, slant left," and "Fade, Tony, look for the fade." I was literally watching Rich Rod signal plays in from the sideline and telling our defense what was coming. This was fun!

Maryland won the game 32–20, and the next week in the *Charleston Gazette*, back in West Virginia, there was an article about former West Virginia quarterback Scott McBrien stealing signals for Maryland. I was now a wanted man in the Mountaineer state.

Maryland was on its way to a huge season. It was great to be part of a winning team, but *part* was the key word. By this time, the coaches and players saw that I had some game, and I had made friends among my teammates, but still I had to drive home every day after school and couldn't dress or participate on game days. Unless you've been in a Division 1 college program, it may be hard to understand what it is like not eat, study, room, travel, and dress on game day with your teammates. The camaraderie, the sense of being in it together, us against them. My exile was teaching me how much this game meant to me, this game that at times I had thought I hated.

In early November, on a Monday after we had clinched a tie for the ACC title with a win over Clemson, I was called into Coach Friedgen's office before practice. I wasn't sure what was up. Had I missed a class assignment? Did I not measure up? Oh no, quite the opposite. Coach told me what a great job I had been doing and offered me a full scholarship.

I left Coach Friedgen's office with a great sense of accomplishment and immediately called my mother with the news. She was thrilled. I was back. Not all the way back just yet, but I was moving into a dorm after Christmas break and would become a full member of a football family once again.

Later that day at practice, Coach Locksley walked by me in the stretch lines and said, "I told you so." We exchanged looks and smiled.

The following Saturday night at Carter-Finley Stadium in Raleigh, Maryland beat North Carolina State by four points, clinching the ACC title. This meant an invitation to the Orange Bowl against Steve Spurrier's Florida Gators, led by Rex Grossman, who would go on to quarterback the Chicago Bears in Super Bowl 41.

Even though I was getting a scholarship next semester, I couldn't travel with the team to South Beach. The final kicker was that I wasn't given any of the bowl gifts—electronics, watches, sports apparel, and a whole treasure trove of goodies. That hurt, as did having to watch the game at home, which Maryland lost 56–23. But it had been a great season for the Terps, who finished with a 10–2 record, and big things were expected for next season, a season to which I was determined to contribute.

During the semester break, the head of football operations asked me if there was anyone I wanted to room with. I mentioned Scooter Monroe, who was a receiver with whom I had practiced during the season. I didn't know him that well, but I knew he was a good guy and someone I would get along with.

Scooter had a single room in Allegany Hall located on the south side of campus, but he agreed, and we crammed my bed into the small space. That showed what type of guy Scooter was, never once complaining. Fortunately for us, a few weeks later a larger room opened up. Back living in the dorm, I once again felt like a complete member of the team. It was a great feeling.

CHAPTER 8

THE GRIND

The team attended winter workouts three days a week at the Armory, an old facility on campus that was a huge gymnasium. Workouts started at six in the morning, and they were tough, not only because we had to get up at such an ungodly hour but also because the conditioning itself was hardcore. Coaches were at different stations where players would do bear crawls, sprints, up-downs, etc., one station after another. It was one hour of nonstop exercise, and it was difficult, more mental than physical. I was back in the grind, but for the first time I was really interacting with all my teammates.

One thing that stood out during winter workouts was a rumor broadcast on ESPN that Coach Friedgen was taking an interview for the head coaching job in the NFL with the Tampa Bay Buccaneers. Dennard Wilson, a defensive back from DeMatha who I had played with and who had already seen plenty of game action for the Terps, called a players' meeting. He said we needed to confront Coach Friedgen and see where he stood. I couldn't believe that Dennard had the courage to do this.

So the next morning at six o'clock, the team was in the Armory in our sweats, all standing off at the far end instead of going to our stations. Coach Friedgen hadn't arrived yet, but the assistant coaches suspected something was up. I'm sure they had been hearing the rumors too.

When Coach Friedgen walked into the Armory, he asked what was going on. Dennard stepped forward and said, "Coach, we all saw on ESPN last night that you have been interviewing for other coaching jobs. Before we go through this workout this morning, all we want to know is, are you in or are you out?"

Silence. You could have heard a pin drop.

"I'm in," Coach Friedgen said. "Now let's get to work."

And that was the last we ever heard of Ralph Friedgen leaving Maryland. I sometimes wonder if at the very moment Dennard confronted Coach, he made his mind up to stay. I will never know, but to this day my teammates and I owe a big thank-you to Dennard for stepping up.

The following week, before morning workout at the Armory, Coach Friedgen called off practice and said we were going to have a team meeting instead. Coach said that former starting quarterback Calvin McCall, who had quit the team last year to concentrate on playing basketball for the Terps, wanted back on the football team.

"I would like your input," Coach said to the team about letting Calvin return.

A couple of players said that since he had quit on us, we shouldn't let him back. But E. J. Henderson, our All-American linebacker and a team leader, said, "I want him back."

Coach said he would think about it. I was worried. Calvin was a gifted athlete, and his rejoining the team could impact my chances of winning the starting job. But two days later, at the next winter workout, Coach announced that he was not letting Calvin rejoin the team. It's hard to say what might have happened if he had let him join, but in the dog-eat-dog world of Division 1 football, I felt as though I had dodged a bullet.

After two months of winter workouts, it was go time—spring ball. Chris Kelley, a top recruit from Seneca Valley High School in Germantown, Maryland, was the number one quarterback entering spring ball. Shaun Hill's backup from last year had been moved to receiver, and I was the number two quarterback. Coach McGregor's prediction about things opening up for me at Maryland was beginning to unfold.

Charlie Taaffe, the offensive coordinator and quarterback coach, told me and Chris that we were competing for the starting position. But Chris had the advantage of knowing the offense, since I had run the scout team last season.

Once again, I had to learn new terminology and a new system. And Coach Friedgen ran a pro-style offense that was more detailed and complex than anything I had previously experienced. We had a list of twenty plays for every situation, such as when we were backed up on the goal line, first and ten, third and three. You name a situation, and we had a comprehensive list of plays for it. My head was swimming with plays, and many of them I wasn't comfortable running, but I kept that to myself. I was fighting for a starting job and didn't want to appear as though I couldn't handle it.

Over the course of the spring, after each practice I began to understand and grasp the offense, little by little. I was growing more comfortable in this system that fit my game of reading a defense, setting up in the pocket, and delivering the ball on time to my receivers. But there were still many nuances to this complex pro-style offense that I needed to master.

And the competition with Chris was close; both of us had solid practices. Chris and I were told that we would split playing time during the spring game. In the first half, we both were playing well, and then early in the second half, Chris tore his ACL. He had previously done this in high school in the Chesapeake Classic All-Star game, and I felt terrible for him. We had become friends, playing golf on a couple of occasions, and though we were competing for a job, we respected each other. I had to finish up the rest of the game at quarterback, and I had a solid outing, throwing a couple of touchdowns and running the offense efficiently.

The offense we ran had been used by Coach Friedgen when he was the offensive coordinator for the San Diego Chargers team that went to Super Bowl 29. Studying tapes of Chargers' games with Coach Friedgen was like taking a master's class in quarterbacking. Ralph Friedgen had an understanding and knowledge of offense that was at another level than any I had been around. Simply put, he was brilliant at the offensive side of the game, especially in teaching the complexities of reading a defense. This was way advanced from high school, where once a defense was set in its position, I could read where the weaknesses were. But in college, the coaches would disguise their defense by having linebackers and defensive backs switching areas at the snap of the ball.

Coach Friedgen constantly told me to read the free safety. "Scott," he would tell me, "the corners lie. The safeties don't lie." The reason was that safeties had too much space to cover. But then I had to learn to read not only a defense before the snap but also after the ball was snapped when they revealed their true coverage. It was a cat-and-mouse game that Coach Friedgen understood inside and out. But for me, it was like taking an honors calculus course.

Over the summer, I attended summer school and participated in the summer strength and conditioning program run by the strength coaches that was similar to West Virginia. One thing that was different from West Virginia was that the skill players played seven-on-seven against some of the local Division 3 schools such as Bowie State and Howard, with the strength coaches officiating.

With Chris doing rehab, I ran all the plays and gained experience working with the receivers, and at the same time they were learning about my game. Just like at DeMatha, playing seven-on-seven against other schools was a blast.

By the time fall camp arrived, Chris Kelley had rehabbed himself back into game condition—an amazing work ethic on his part. Coach Taaffe told us that we were still competing for the starting job. And it was so close that in the third week of August, Coach Friedgen told the *Washington Post* that he might use a platoon system at quarterback. I had been through that my sophomore year at Good Counsel and wanted nothing to do with a platoon system, which never allowed me to get into a rhythm.

It was a hard-fought battle between Chris and I, but a week before camp, I was given the starting job.

Chapter 9

MATURATION OF A QUARTERBACK

Now that I had won the starting job, it was up to me to keep it. Our opening game would present a challenge. We were playing Notre Dame in New Jersey at the Meadowlands on Saturday night, primetime, in front of a national audience on ABC.

Leading up to the game, there was a lot of hoopla and excitement on campus and among the players. This was big-time college football, and it was on a stage that proved to be more than I could handle. We got beaten soundly 22–0, and I had a horrible game: nine for twenty-three with two interceptions.

During the game, I was unsure of my reads at the line of scrimmage and unsure of myself. I felt a step slow not just physically but mentally as well. It got so bad that I was pulled in the second half, and Chris came in. He didn't do much either: three for nine with a pick.

It had been two years since I had competed in a game that counted, and the speed of it was something I couldn't handle. It was as though the moment had been too big for me. I was disappointed in myself and felt that I had let down not only my team but also all the hometown fans. Playing football at the University of Maryland had been my dream since childhood, and now I had failed both in front of friends and family, as well was on national television and one of the biggest stages in college football.

Sunday was a miserable day off. I made the mistake of turning on ESPN and watching the lowlights of me getting intercepted and sacked. I compounded it by reading the sports page of the *Washington Post*, which in its coverage of the game wrote, "New quarterback Scott McBrien couldn't generate any offense and was hesitant in running the option." True enough, but I felt that I was being singled out as the reason we lost, and to read it in a major newspaper like the *Washington Post* only confirmed that I had failed.

Coach Friedgen ran the quarterback film session, and he held nothing back. He critiqued my mistakes with no-holds-barred honesty, continually telling me that cornerbacks lie and safeties don't. Reading the defense after I took the ball from under center was hard for me to grasp. Players were flying around everywhere, and I had so much going on in my mind that it was hard to think clearly, much less try to understand what the defensive backs were doing. At this point, I wasn't sure if I was still the starter or not.

Before our first practice, Coach Taaffe told me and Chris that the starting job was open, and we would be competing during the week for playing the following Saturday at home against Akron.

On Thursday after our last practice before the game, Charlie Taaffe told me I would be starting on Saturday.

Against Akron I ran and threw for a touchdown. We won 44–14. I didn't have to throw the ball much, as our running game and the defense were operating on all cylinders, but I ran the offense efficiently without a turnover, though I was still not comfortable reading the defense after the snap.

The next game was against perennial power Florida State, the bully boy of the ACC. As usual, they were loaded with talent and speed all over the field. Maryland had never beaten Florida State. Even the last year when the Terps won the ACC, they had lost to the Seminoles.

I was nervous all week going into the game, oftentimes finding it hard to focus during practice and film sessions. The big moment was getting to me. I feared another debacle like the Notre Dame game.

My fears became reality, as the game was a repeat of Notre Dame but worse. I was terrible, fourteen for twenty-six with two interceptions. Chris came in during the second half and didn't do any better, six for eleven with two interceptions.

Once again, I felt miserable and questioned whether I was good enough. Coach Friedgen's impersonal quote in the Sunday sports page of the *Washington Post* summed up my tenuous position: "I don't think the quarterback played good."

After two miserable nights of restless sleep, I went to my Monday morning classes, and as I walked from class to class, I was certain everyone knew who I was and how I had let the entire school down with dismal performances against Notre Dame and now Florida State. By the end of my last class, I called my mother and I told her I didn't want to go to practice and wanted to quit football. I couldn't take it any longer.

"Not again!" my mother said. "You're not quitting, Scott. You've been doing this since Maplewood. You are going to stick it out at Maryland." After some more back-and-forth, she told me to hold fast and said she was leaving work to meet with me.

We drove around campus. Students hustled and bustled around us, and I thought how nice it would be to be like them, with only school to worry about. My mother parked the car in front of the chapel on the south side of campus, away from things. There was something so solemn about the tall white steeple and the white columns. It was as though I was facing a moment of truth.

I looked at my mother, tears welling in my eyes. "I can't take it, Mom. I can't do it. It's too much." I continued to vent about the media's scrutiny and whether I was good enough to play for Maryland.

"Scott, you have overcome obstacles at every level of football you've ever played at and succeeded," she said as she put her hand on my shoulder. "In the end it's your decision, but why should this be any different?"

To this day, I'm not sure if my mother made a phone call, but Mike Locksley called me into his office and told me that he knew it was tough with the media pounding me but that I needed to stay positive and we'd work our way through it. "I know you're good enough, Scott, to succeed at this level," were his final words. With a pat on the shoulder, he escorted me to the door. Having Coach Locksley reaffirming his belief in me meant a lot, since up to this point, I had not shown anyone that I was a Division 1 caliber quarterback.

During the week, Chris and I once again competed for the starting job.

I had a solid week of practice, putting last week's debacle behind me, and after Thursday's practice, Coach Friedgen told me I would be starting Saturday.

Our next two games were against lesser opponents Eastern Michigan and Wofford, both of which we won handily. In the game against Eastern Michigan, I threw for three hundred yards and three touchdowns. One play that stood out was when I threw an eighty-yard touchdown to my go-to guy and roommate, Scooter Monroe, but it got called back for holding. The very next play, I threw the same pass to Steve Suter for a ninety-yard touchdown. It was that kind of day.

After two consecutive wins, I was now the starting quarterback, but I sensed that the team was waiting for me to break out against a challenging opponent.

As fate would have it, next on our schedule we were heading to West Virginia to take on Rich Rod and the Mountaineers. This was a huge game for both schools. Besides being border rivals, after this game, each team would go into the heart of their conference schedule. A win against a strong opponent would provide momentum. A loss, well, I didn't even want to consider that as a possibility. Besides wanting to beat my old coach and teammates, we had more talent.

A big adjustment was made during the week in practice when Coach Taaffe had me run our option package from the shotgun instead of taking the snap from behind center. "When the time is right," Coach Taaffe told me in the quarterback meeting, "we're going to have you read the defensive end from the shotgun. If he holds his position, Scott, hand it off to the runner. But if he crashes the back, keep the ball and scoot around the end."

I immediately felt more comfortable making my read from the shotgun and being able to see the entire defense. It seemed like a small thing, but running the shotgun in a spread offense changed the course of my football career.

For this big game, I felt ready for the challenge. No more uncertainty about my ability. I was going to play in a place I was familiar with and against a group of players whose tendencies I knew inside and out. In a way, it was a blessing in disguise to return to Morgantown for a chance to prove myself against a worthy opponent in a hostile environment.

That Monday, going out onto the practice field, Coach Locksley came up beside me and said through an emerging grin, "Gonna visit your old boys from the hills this weekend."

I replied, "Coach Locks, it's not about that."

He winked at me as if we were sharing a secret. "Oh yeah it is, Scotty."

Coach Locksley was always encouraging players in his own casual way, but behind it was the heart of a man who cared deeply about us not only as players but also as people. Every team needs a Coach Locks.

Approaching the practice field, I saw six big speakers on tall stands around the field. I wasn't sure what that was about.

After warm-ups, I huddled with the offense and came to the line of scrimmage against the scout team. As I began to call out the play, a song blared out of the speakers: "Almost heaven, West Virginia ..."

From my time as a Mountaineer, I knew that song by heart. It was John Denver singing "Take Me Home, Country Road."

I couldn't believe it. Coach Locksley was screaming at me, "This is your song, Scotty. We gonna visit your old boys from the hills." I stepped back from center and couldn't help but crack up laughing, as did the rest of my teammates, who were screaming out, "Yeehaw, it's Scott's song."

It was a great move on Coach Friedgen's part, for it not only loosened up the team, but it also let me know I had the support of my coaches and teammates for this game.

During practice that week, Coach Friedgen was on my case, yelling at me for every little mishap on my part, but I never let it get to me. I didn't perceive it like the wild rants I had endured with Coach Rodriguez. It's funny to look back on it now. Coach Friedgen could really upset some of my teammates with his harangues, but after dealing with Rich Rod, it never bothered me.

This all came to a head later in the week when I threw a pass late to a receiver over the middle and Coach Friedgen stopped practice and, clutching his ever-present clipboard, began screaming at me. "McBrien, if you throw late across the middle one more time, I will run you until your heart stops."

I was in the huddle with the offense, trying to call the next play, and Coach Friedgen came storming up to the rear of the huddle and hollered in my ear, "Do you understand me, McBrien?"

I looked up at my huddled teammates and smiled nice and easy, as if I didn't have a care in the world. There was a collective look of awe in their eyes, as if they couldn't believe this wasn't getting to me, and in the shadows of their gaze was a newfound look of respect. A look that said, *Our quarterback has some cojones. Big ones.*

That was the last time Coach Friedgen ever went ballistic on me. I think he had been testing me all along to see if I could take it and to prepare me for what he expected I would receive from a packed house in Morgantown. And part of the reason, Coach Friedgen's tirades never got to me was the fact that they never seemed personal, more like a gruff uncle who went off every now and then.

All week leading up to the game, Coach Friedgen would not allow the media to speak with me. I think he was worried, not so much that I would say the wrong thing, but he didn't want me answering a lot of questions over my return to West Virginia. He was trying to keep me as calm and focused as possible. He knew this game was as important to me as it was for the entire team.

On Friday, the team took the three-and-a-half-hour bus ride from College Park to Morgantown. Coach Friedgen had me sit next to him for the entire trip, picking my brain about West Virginia's tendencies and formations and going over the entire game plan with me. While my teammates zoned out, napping or listening to music over headphones, I spent an exhausting session in the classroom with the head coach.

But mentally, I was in a good place. Coach Friedgen and his staff had prepared me with an excellent game plan to attack the Mountaineer defense. "If they're in a three-three stack, Scott," Coach Friedgen had told me every day in film session that week, "and the DB comes to the line, look for Jafar in the flat." Or he told me if the defensive backs stay back, I should call the run. The game plan was to run the ball until they changed their defense by bringing more men to the line. Then we would pass. Simple reads, but as it turned out, effective ones.

I was confident in understanding the Mountaineer schemes and knowing the tendencies of the players behind them. What they liked to do in certain situations, who was strong in coverage, who was weak in pursuit—all the little traits that I had practiced against for two years were now a big asset in my favor.

We stayed at a hotel on the outskirts of Morgantown, and throughout team meetings, meals, and walk-throughs in a conference room, I maintained an aura of calmness. My teammates seemed to pick up on this, as if to say, *If Scott isn't worried about this game, then we're okay.* It wasn't anything I was doing intentionally, just that I seemed to be exuding a sense of preparedness, of being ready for this very big moment in my life.

Saturday morning, we departed the hotel for Mountaineer Field. When we entered the parking lot, little kids flipped us the bird, adults threw batteries and eggs at the bus, and everyone screamed and yelled at us. Welcome to Mountaineer football. But I had seen this act before. Many of my teammates had never experienced such a wild scene entering a stadium, and once again they seemed to pick up on my relaxed state of confidence, as if they were saying, *If it isn't bothering Scott, then it sure isn't gonna bother me.*

Also, this was a chance to show Rich Rodriguez what he had missed in a quarterback, and I was so looking forward to playing against my old friends.

When we went onto the field for pregame warm-ups—jerseys with no pads—the student section was packed. There was nary an empty seat. When they spotted me, they began a sing-song chant: "F ... McBrien ... F ... McBrien."

On and on it went. But little did those students know that instead of upsetting me, it made me all the more determined to show them my A game. When my teammates came up to me to offer words of encouragement, it sent a chill down my spine that I still remember to this day. Game on.

As all the commotion was going on, Steve Suter, one of my receivers, said to me, "Isn't that a beautiful chant? We got your back today, McBee." Suter always called me McBee. He then ran over to the Mountaineer student section and raised his arms as if to say, *Louder.* Steve Suter was a one-of-a-kind player and teammate. That moment was the first time

I felt the team rally behind me. It was as if they were saying, *You're our quarterback. You're our guy.*

Before we returned to the field for the opening kickoff, Steve Suter and Rich Parson, also a receiver, called me to the front of the line and told me to lead the team out of the tunnel.

As I led the Terps out, I was greeted by sixty-five thousand strong booing me with a vengeance. It was one of the coolest moments of my football career. *Yeah, bring it on!*

In the stands I had a contingent of family and friends, including my mother and Katie, uncles, aunts, and cousins. My family knew how important this game was to me and also to them.

After we received the kickoff, I came on the field, and once again I heard a thunderous roar of boos. The return of the prodigal son.

On the opening drive, we moved the ball right down the field. From West Virginia's twenty yard line, I set up in the shotgun, put the ball in the belly of my tailback Chris Downs, saw the end lunge for Chris, and pulled the ball out of Chris's belly. The defense made a beeline toward Chris, leaving me all alone, just like Coach Taaffe had envisioned when he drew up the play.

As I scooted around the right end, I had nothing but open spaces and the end zone ahead of me, save for my old roommate and good friend, Brian King, playing cornerback. Jafar Williams blocked him toward the center of the field, allowing me to run free toward the end zone.

As I neared the goal line, in my excitement, I tripped and ended up somersaulting forward in the end zone. I bounced up as my teammates greeted me in celebration. But when I came to the sidelines and put on the headphones to talk to Coach Taaffe up in the press box, he reamed me out for hotdogging in the end zone. I tried to explain that I tripped, but he didn't buy it until Monday when we watched the film and both had a good laugh about it. But during the game, he was mad because he was worried about a fifteen-yard penalty for unsportsmanlike conduct.

Later in the first quarter, I was sacked by defensive tackle David Upchurch, a big old guy who was always talking smack to people. As he was on top of me, he screamed into my helmet, "Scott, you are so ugly. So damn ugly."

I yelled right back, "Me? Look in the mirror. You fat. And you ugly." Now, this was all in good fun, just football players being football players, and it loosened me up. Two plays later, I threw a perfect fifty-yard bomb to Jafar Williams for a touchdown. And the man defending on the play was Brian King.

The game ended up Maryland 48 and West Virginia 7. Coach Friedgen and Coach Taaffe's game plan had been on the money. It was a sweet win, very sweet. After the game I was greeted by many of my old teammates, Brian King among them. They all wished me good luck. I never saw Coach Rodriguez.

Outside the locker room, on the way to our bus to head back home, I saw my family. There were hugs all around. My cousin Shannon Morris told me she had been so worried for me all week and then because of all the belligerent swearing directed at me before kickoff. "Scott," she said to me with a big hug, "when you scored your first touchdown, that was the best thirty seconds of my life, and this is the greatest day of my life."

On the bus ride home, I had a grin on my face that just would not go away. Neither would the thought in my mind that this was the beginning of my college career as a quarterback.

Chapter 10

HONING MY GAME

Next on our schedule was a Thursday night game at home against Georgia Tech. ESPN covered the game with Mike Tirico, Kirk Herbstreit, and Lee Corso in the booth. This was a week that came to be known by me and my teammates as Sniper Week.

For three weeks in October, the entire Washington, DC, metropolitan area was in a state of fear. As it turned out, two men were driving around shooting and killing innocent people at gas stations and the Home Depot. Nowhere seemed safe. They even shot a boy in front of his elementary school in Bowie, Maryland, not far from campus. Each day it seemed like a new victim was killed or wounded.

That week of practice, the team was on edge, and I was especially nervous standing out in the only yellow jersey—quarterbacks were not allowed to be hit—during drills.

Before the game, I noticed a TV cameraman sitting up on his platform but with a new twist. He had a wooden barrier on three sides to protect him from a rifle shot. The security for the game was tight, and there was an added edginess in the stands and among my teammates.

This was the only game on TV that night, and back then it was a big deal. I had a solid game, connecting on some long passes to Scooter, and we won, going away 34–10.

Every Monday after a game, Coach Friedgen, who little by little was gaining more confidence in me, gave me more freedom in my play calling (checking out of plays at the line of scrimmage) and added more wrinkles to the offense by expanding my repertoire of plays.

Our next two games were on the road. First up, we rolled over Duke 45–12. Next, we faced the North Carolina Tar Heels in Chapel Hill, where Steve Suter got us great field position by running back the opening kickoff to the fifty yard line. On the first play from scrimmage, I threw a curl route to a wide-open Scooter, but he dropped the ball. I didn't say a word to him in the huddle. Instead, I shot him a look. Scooter dropped his head. Point made. It was the type of scolding look a friend could give to a friend. Someone I didn't know as well might have taken it the wrong way.

After that it was smooth sailing as Scooter and I connected on three long passes for 167 yards, and our running game ran roughshod over their defense, as we won 59–7. We were on a roll, and I was now without question the starting quarterback. Not only that, but I was emerging as one of the team leaders, and later the next week Coach Friedgen made me a team captain.

I was honored, but for me, being a captain wasn't so much about giving pep talks—that wasn't me—but more in the way I carried myself and led by example. Showing up for everything on time, studying my game plan, being prepared at film sessions with Charlie Taaffe—all of this allowed me to get players in the right positions and to command the offense with confidence. The confidence I emitted was picked up loud and clear by my teammates.

The following Saturday at noon, a very good North Carolina State came to College Park, led by their stud quarterback, Phillip Rivers. A couple of minutes into the second quarter, we were down 14–0 as Rivers was throwing darts on the money and their running game was effective enough to keep our defense honest.

We came back on a sixty-four-yard reverse run by Steve Suter for a touchdown. Game on. It went back and forth, including me faking a hand off up the middle and running a naked bootleg around left end for a twenty-six-yard touchdown. There was nobody in sight. Thank you, Joe LaPietra, for teaching me the proper technique on the play fake at Maplewood.

We secured victory right at the end, and after I downed the ball to end the game, the student section rushed the field, tearing down the goal post—a first for me. We had now won seven games in a row, and North

Carolina State's coach, Chuck Amato, said after the game that we were the hottest team in the conference.

This was my first season in college as a full-time starter, and it was both physically and mentally taxing. Besides football, I was carrying fifteen hours of class work. A normal day for me began by attending mandatory breakfast in the players' dining hall at seven thirty and then taking two or three classes. Then came lunch, reporting to the practice facility to get taped, watching a film session with Charlie Taaffe and the other quarterbacks from three thirty to four thirty, and then practicing until six thirty. After practice the entire team had to trudge all the way across campus to the dining hall on the south end, eat dinner, and then return to our rooms for homework, only to repeat it all over again to the next day. With that schedule, there was little time for anything else during the season.

One would think that, being the starting quarterback on a nationally ranked team, I would draw some attention walking around campus. But I wasn't big or muscular like many of my teammates, and I melded right into the student body. Very few people seemed to recognize me in College Park, and that was fine with me. I had enough on my plate without a lot of hoopla.

By our last game of the season, we were 9–3 and there was a trip to the Peach Bowl in Atlanta on New Year's Eve at stake if we won at home against Wake Forest. We took care of business, beating the Demon Deacons 32–14, and I had one of my better games, going seventeen for twenty-eight and throwing for 275 yards and two touchdowns.

CHAPTER 11

THE PEACH BOWL

Maryland's selection to play in the Peach Bowl was important for me. Last season, I had been on the scout team and watched the Terps play in the Orange Bowl from my living room. Now, not only was I a member of the team, but I was a main cog in the offense. Our opponent was Tennessee from the SEC, considered by many to be the best football conference in the country. Maryland had not won a bowl game in seventeen years, and a win would do wonders, and not just for team morale; it could boost the fan base and something else very important—help with recruiting.

But the Volunteers were a strong team with a quality quarterback in four-year starter Casey Clausen, along with his superb tight end Jason Witten, who would go on to have a great career for the Dallas Cowboys. The Vols had eight other players on the roster who would get selected in the 2003 NFL draft.

When we arrived at the Marriott Marquis in Atlanta, it was beginning to sink in how far I had come. The hotel was incredible: The atrium, one of the largest in the world, spanned the entire height of the fifty-two-story building and consisted of two vertical chambers divided by elevator shafts and bridges. And there was a players' lounge in the hotel with a ton of arcade and board games.

The best part was waiting for us in the lounge: bowl gifts, including video cameras, gym bags, backpacks, shoes, and hoodies. We loved it. Many of my teammates came from hardscrabble backgrounds and the looks on their faces was like that of kids on Christmas day.

The week leading up to the game was a whirlwind of events. Besides practicing daily at Georgia Tech, we visited hospitals and engaged in joint luncheons and dinners with Tennessee, where the players were joined by family and friends. It was a blast.

The practices were the same, except there was little hitting. I was told by players who had gone to last year's Orange Bowl that this was a change. Coach Friedgen had worked the team out in full pads in the Miami heat with loads of contact, and the Terps had been blown out by Florida. This year he was applying a different tactic.

The game was played at the Georgia Dome, home to the Atlanta Falcons, on ESPN. Maryland was outnumbered in fan support. At one end of the stadium were the Maryland fans dressed in red. But the remainder of the eighty-thousand-seat structure was predominantly Tennessee orange. All week, everywhere my teammates and I went, we heard the Tennessee band playing the team fight song, "Rocky Top." We heard it at the battle of the bands, at team events, and anywhere that we engaged with the Tennessee team.

Besides being outnumbered in fans and band presence, Maryland was a one-point underdog in the game, which seemed like a home game for Tennessee with the stadium packed in a sea of orange.

But my teammates and I were focused on one thing only—winning. We received the ball first and drove down the field to their one yard line, facing a fourth down. The play signaled in was for me to hand off to Bruce Perry up the middle. But during the drive, I had noticed that the defensive end had not been paying attention to me when I handed off on previous plays where I would fake the naked bootleg around the end, running it out just as I had been taught by Joe LaPietra at Maplewood.

All my teammates thought it was a run for Bruce, but after breaking the huddle, I decided that I was going to keep this one myself. After the snap, I jerked the ball out of Bruce's belly and ran around the end, untouched, into the end zone. We went on to win the game handily, 30–3, with me scoring on another short run. And the best part was I never heard their fight song, "Rocky Top," for the remainder of the trip.

After the game, a stage was rolled out to the center of the field, and a representative from the bowl committee told me that I was the offensive MVP of the game. E. J. Henderson, our great middle linebacker, who had a monster game with three sacks and a forced fumble, was the defensive MVP.

Standing on that stage, holding the enormous Peach Bowl MVP trophy—a golden football atop a glass plaque that was secured to a heavy wood-trimmed base—was a moment I will always remember. Just a year before, I had been sitting at home with my mother and sister, bummed out, watching the Terps get trounced in the Orange Bowl. Now I was holding the MVP trophy with the Maryland fans cheering and millions of people watching me on television. It was one of the wow moments in my life, and I couldn't have asked for a better way to spend New Years Eve.

Back at the hotel, in the glass elevator, I held the trophy up to an atrium full of Maryland fans cheering me. But the best moment was when I got to my mother's room and showed her the trophy. The look in her eyes said it all. It was a look of more than just pride in a son but also of relieved joy. Her boy had persevered through it all. Of course, she had persevered right along with me, every step of the way on my journey to become a starting Division 1 quarterback.

In recognition of my quarterback play during the season, I was awarded the Golden Helmet by the Touchdown Club of Annapolis. This was a prestigious black-tie event where I had an opportunity to meet such quarterbacking legends as Roger Staubach and Peyton Manning.

One funny incident during this event was when my presenter, Tim Strachan, who had been a nationally top three ranked quarterback going into his senior year at DeMatha—the same year as Peyton Manning— was talking to Peyton and mentioned that he was friends with the Maryland quarterback who had won an award.

Peyton said he had heard good things about me and asked where I was. Tim pointed to me standing nearby, having overheard the entire conversation. "That's him?" Peyton said in a tone of disbelief: *That little guy?* I laughed to myself. Instead of taking it as a slight, I took it as a compliment that someone of my stature had played at the level I had.

Tim called me over and introduced me to Peyton, who was all of his listed height of six feet five. Peyton told me that one bit of advice he would give about quarterbacking was that when all else fails, checkdown. That means if you approach the line and nothing looks available for the play called, you can always bail out on a short pass to a back in the flat. And it crossed my mind that I had been doing checkdowns not only on the field but also off the field, and I had ended up as the starting quarterback for the Maryland Terrapins, with another year ahead of me.

Chapter 12

CHANGES

It had been a successful season, with a 11–3 record, a bowl victory, and the Terps ranked thirteenth in the country. But it had been a long and exhausting run. I was physically beat up and mentally exhausted. But I had little time to relax because I had to take classes during winter term, which was a truncated semester between fall and spring semesters when the campus was mostly empty. But this was part of the deal of playing Division 1 football, which was like a full-time job. Defensive back Josh Wilson had a quote in the newspaper that summed it up: "It's not fun and games. It really takes a toll on your mind if you don't love it."

Part of the job was the inevitable changes that took place. One was losing good players to graduation, such as my center, Todd Wike; one of our tailbacks, Chris Downs; my good buddy Scooter Monroe; and our all-American linebacker E. J. Henderson, who was drafted in the second round by the Minnesota Vikings and would go on to an standout nine-year NFL career.

But a huge loss to me and many of my teammates was running back coach Mike Locksley leaving to take a job at the University of Florida. Coach Locksley had recruited me in high school and was instrumental in my transferring to Maryland from West Virginia. He was like a big brother to many of the players, a young guy you could go to and talk to about anything.

But for the 2003 season, we were loaded with up-and-coming underclassmen like linebackers Shawn Merriman and D'Qwell Jackson, tight end Vernon Davis, defensive lineman Randy Starks, cornerback

Dominique Foxworth, and kicker Nick Novak—special athletes who would all go on to star in the NFL.

The same was true for the coaching staff, especially on offense with our brilliant head coach, Ralph Friedgen; offensive coordinator, Charlie Taaffe, who was a excellent coach and all-around good guy; the wide receiver coach and recruiting coordinator James Franklin, a young and up-and-coming coach who combined a high football IQ with relentless energy; and our newest addition, Coach Bill O'Brien, who replaced Mike Locksley and would go on to become head coach of the Houston Texans. All of this added up to a positive vibe and a confident energy among the players during winter workouts that carried over to spring ball.

During spring ball and into the off-season, I was becoming the face of Maryland football. I was on the cover of ACC and Maryland football magazines and had my own billboards on the side of highways.

Also, I was beginning to draw attention from the local media and was becoming the go-to player for quotes by newspapers, radio, and television.

In a big article on me in the *Washington Post*, written by Barry Svrluga, I said I had put my departure from West Virginia behind me and that it was over and done with, but my mother made her feelings known indirectly by saying in reference to the Maryland coaching staff, "They knew how to coach and teach without making a kid feel like he's no good. They don't belittle you and make you feel like you're never going to make it."

But I never let any of the press coverage go to my head; though I was beginning to get recognized here and there out in public, it was nothing to the extent I would have if I had stayed in Morgantown, which lived Mountaineer football 24-7. At Maryland and in the surrounding DC area, there were plenty of other options for sports entertainment.

But my growing fame for the upcoming 2003 season almost crash landed when, during winter workouts sessions, a big snow storm hit and all school activities were shut down. Scooter and I and a few other players took dates to one of the local establishments, R.J. Bentley's. Bentley's, as we called it, was a sports bar with jerseys of famous Maryland athletes hanging on the walls. It was a friendly, comfortable place where all the athletes from the different teams liked to go and unwind.

We had a good old time, drinking a few beers with friends. As we came out of the bar, we saw one lone car puttering down Route 1 in the snow, going about five miles an hour. Mike Whaley, a linebacker—yes, of course, it had to be a linebacker—decided to roll across the hood of the car as if he had been hit: a practical joke.

But it was bitterly cold, and big old Mike, in rolling across the hood, cracked the windshield. With that, five fraternity guys got out of the car and went after Mike, who had no choice but to defend himself.

In a flash, Scooter jumped into the fray like some action-figure hero. He was throwing guys off Mike, onto the sidewalk, and into the side of the car like they were straw men. Before I even had a chance to consider getting involved, Scooter had cleaned house in no time while I stood on the sidewalk with our dates, in awe of what I had just seen. *Scooter, my man? Who knew?*

Then a town cop walked up to me and said, "Scott, I know who you are. Walk away." I escorted our dates across a side street and watched as Scooter told the policeman that the other guys had started it, and when the dust had settled, no charges were filed. Lesson learned. I had to be careful about avoiding situations like that. If things had gone another way, such as me jumping into the fight and someone getting injured, my collegiate football career could have ended.

CHAPTER 13

EXPECTATIONS

During two-a-days before my senior season, there were big expectations for the Maryland football team from the press, fans, and alumni. I was expected to not only perform up to my standards last year but improve upon them. There was some big-time pressure resting squarely on my shoulders.

The entire team was staying in freshman dorms right near the stadium, and every day, Steve Suter and I walked back and forth from the practice field to our temporary dining hall. Steve could always read me like a book, and he seemed to sense that I was feeling the strain of the upcoming season.

Along our path was a crab apple tree. Steve would pick an apple off the tree and say, "McBee, I want you to hit that stop sign."

I'd wind up and let it rip and nail the sign dead center. Steve would holler, "Bing! Oh yeah, McBee." On our way back from practice, Steve would hand me another crab apple. "McBee, I want you to hit that light pole." I'd wind up again and nail that pole dead center, exploding the apple.

This became a routine, sort of a little take-your-mind-off-things drill that we both started looking forward to. My accuracy was so uncanny that when Steve told me to hit a telephone wire hanging between two poles, so help me, I split that apple right between the wire. It got to the point that Steve started thinking we could make money taking bets on my ability to throw a crab apple. It was little things like this that broke the monotony and pressurized restlessness of training camp.

But before we even opened the season at Northern Illinois, I pulled my groin during camp, and I wasn't sure if I would be able to play in the opener. Making matters worse, Suter and our top running back, Bruce Perry, were ruled out from the game at the last moment with minor injuries, as was starting guard, Lamar Bryant, who would be out longer with a broken foot and would be sorely missed for his standout blocking.

Coach Friedgen had emphasized not to overlook this game. He'd harped to his team and the press all week before the game that Northern Illinois was a quality and experienced opponent.

My groin injury prevented me from practicing the week leading up to the game—not the way I envisioned the start to my final season as a Terp. But on the sidelines during practice, I was mentally taking notes as I followed the pass plays and coverages.

Standing next to Coach Taaffe, I noticed the safety coming toward the line. "Safety gonna blitz, Coach."

I looked at Coach Taaffe, and his eyes said, *And?*

"When he's down low, the coverage is going to rotate the opposite way, right?"

We exchange looks. Charlie Taaffe's eyes seemed to smile in approval.

"So," I said, "I got a soft corner over that way."

Coach Taaffe glowed. "You got it. You got it."

And get it, I did. I now had a solid understanding of Coach Friedgen's offense. All I had to do was execute it to the fullest of my ability.

We went into the season opener with a preseason rank of fifteenth in the country. Though Northern Illinois was a mid-major school, they had an excellent team that would go on to beat number twenty-one Alabama, number twenty-three Bowling Green, and Iowa State later that year. This was no cakewalk opener.

Right before kickoff, I told Coach Friedgen I felt good enough to give it a go at playing. On the opening drive, we drove down the field, mixing a few passes with some solid running by Josh Allen, who took it in for the score. But from that point on, it was a nightmarish dogfight. Northern Illinois was a good, solid team, but we continued to shoot ourselves in the foot with missed assignments, turnovers, dropped passes—one would have been a touchdown—missed tackles, and stupid penalties at critical junctures in the game, such as roughing the passer.

The game went into overtime, tied 13–13.

Northern Illinois scored on their opening drive, and then we took over on offense on their twenty-five yard line. The game ended when I threw a fourth-and-goal corner route in the back of the end zone intended for Latrez Harrison. Both Latrez and his defender went up for the pass, which caused the ball to be deflected into the air, resulting in another defender intercepting the pass. There was an obvious interference, as the cornerback had been draped all over Latrez, but it wasn't called, and next thing I knew, people were storming the field in celebration. It was one of the low points of my college career to have to walk off the field among a pack of delirious Northern Illinois fans. I had such a bitter taste of defeat in my mouth.

We had little time to lick our wounds, since our next game was at Florida State, and as usual, they were loaded with speed and talent. The game started out great for us, as D'Qwell Jackson intercepted a pass and rumbled and stumbled it back fifty yards for a touchdown.

We followed that with another drive and a field goal to go up 10–0. But the rest was like an avalanche as Florida State began to score, and I couldn't get anything going. I ended up going six for eighteen for sixty-one yards with one interception. I was pulled late in the second half when the game got out of hand, and we ended up losing 35–10.

After the game, Chick Hernandez from Comcast Sports interviewed me, and I told him that the loss was on me. I hadn't performed the way I needed to play, and that was on my shoulders.

The mood on the team was disappointment, but the other team leaders and I kept reinforcing to our teammates that it was a long season and we shouldn't let it get us down. Of course, this is all cliché, but still, it needed to be said.

Next game we stomped a weak Citadel team 61–0 at home. We had a long way to go in the season, but it still felt good to get a win before our next opponent, West Virginia, came to town.

Once again, Coach Friedgen would not allow me to speak to the media the week leading up to the game. The Mountaineers had a good team, ranked in the top twenty-five, but I still knew their defense like the back of my hand. Many of my old teammates still played on the team, and I was looking forward to playing them. In a way, it wasn't fair, because I knew their tendencies so well—a big advantage. We beat them good: 34–7. I had a solid game going fourteen for twenty-five for 220 yards and also ran for forty-seven yards. One thing that stood out to me in this game was a young cocky cornerback named Adam Jones—later to be known as Pacman Jones—who would go on to become a quality NFL cornerback. He wasn't very tall and was guarding Latrez Harrison, who at six feet two had a big size advantage over the five-feet-nine Jones.

By this time, Coach Friedgen had given me free rein to call an audible at the line of scrimmage. And when I saw this little short guy covering Latrez one-on-one, I called the same pass play three times to Latrez in the end zone. And all three times, Adam Jones leapt high into the air and batted the ball down. Adam Jones was the real deal—fast, strong, and lightning quick.

After the win, we felt momentum shifting in our favor; we were beginning to regain our confidence, because in beating the Mountaineers, we had won over a quality opponent.

Next up we had to travel to Ypsilanti to play Eastern Michigan in a game in which we were heavily favored. The Eagles stadium was small—twenty-five-thousand capacity—and the locker rooms reminded me of high school. Playing in front of what appeared to be no more than five thousand spectators was quite a comedown from primetime national television in front of eighty thousand. And though we shouldn't have let our surroundings get to us, we did. I felt, and I could sense my teammates felt it also, that this entire setting was rinky-dink. *Whatever are we doing up here?* It was like we were back in high school.

To me, the best part of a college football game was when my teammates and I ran out onto the field, wearing our school colors, with the smell and chill of autumn in the air. The excitement of the large crowd—home or away—brought a sense of living in the moment, a big and special moment in my life. And now, playing before such a sparse crowd, it felt like all the air had been released from our balloon of enthusiasm.

Our play in the first half was indicative of us allowing our environment affect our play on the field. We led 16–10 going in for halftime, and Coach Friedgen reamed us out in no uncertain terms. I had never seen him so mad, and that was saying something for "The

Fridge," as he had affectionately come to be known. He was red-faced and irate, banging on lockers and kicking over chairs. Well, the big guy got our attention, as we got out of there with a win, 37–13.

The next week, we were back in the big time, playing a three-thirty game on ESPN at home against Clemson and their star quarterback, Charlie Whitehurst. It was a total team win, 21–7, with me throwing three touchdowns. One neat thing about this game was that Tim Brant—a former Terp player and father of my good buddy from Maplewood, Kevin—was announcing the game and gave a shout out to me and Maplewood Football. Also, Boomer Esiason, the former great quarterback, was on the sidelines for the Terps. Boomer had worn number seven, just as I had and both of us were southpaws. Pretty cool.

By this point in the season, I had developed a very close friendship with Steve Suter, who was a standout athlete—fast and quick with great cutting ability. Steve was a threat anytime he got his hands on the ball, especially in the return game. And besides our friendship off the field, we had developed chemistry on the field. Steve was what I liked to call a backyard ballplayer. If a pass route wasn't going to work, he would adjust his route just enough to find open space. And I had a feel for when he was going to do this, and we both seemed to sense what the other was going to do.

Besides being a quality player, Steve Suter was a character. During a practice that final season, we were running a two-minute drill, which was a big deal to the offense and defense because whoever lost the drill had to run sprints at the end of practice. So I faked like I was going to down the ball to stop the clock but turned around with my back to the line of scrimmage and bounced the ball off the ground back up to myself, caught it, wheeled around, and threw a deep touchdown pass down the sideline to Suter.

Then out of the blue, Suter pulled a Sharpie out of his sock, raced back to the offense, and started to sign all of our helmets in celebration. All the while, the coaches were arguing whether the play was legal or not. Later, I found out from a referee that the play was legal, but the coaches decided on a do-over. Game situations like that, along with a personality like Suter, made the drudgery of practice more bearable.

The following week, we beat Duke at home 33–20, in a game that wasn't as close as the score might indicate, as they scored a couple of garbage time touchdowns at the end of the game.

Another game on ESPN down at Georgia Tech was next up. This game turned out to be a low-scoring affair, and in the second quarter with no score, I took a big hit on a quarterback option play. A linebacker hit me helmet to helmet, which is now a penalty. In the moment of impact, I saw stars briefly before crashing onto my backside. I took a moment, got up, and called the huddle. We finished the drive with a field goal, but when I headed toward the sidelines, I became dizzy.

I went to Matt Charvat, one of our trainers, who had me sit on the bench. He did an examination of my head and eyes and then asked me where the locker room was. I could understand the question but didn't know the direction. Then he asked me to remember three words. *Dog, cat, car.* Three minutes later, he returned and asked me to repeat the three words. I could not for the life of me remember. He took my helmet. I was done playing for the day.

We ended up losing 7–3 in a game we should have never lost. Watching game tapes the next week, I didn't remember any of the plays I was involved in during the drive in which I was concussed.

Later in the week, I was cleared to play in the upcoming homecoming game against North Carolina. At the Thursday team meeting before practice, Coach Friedgen told us we'd had a good mental week of practice, meaning players knew their assignments. The Fridge hated mental mistakes; physical mistakes he understood, but not being prepared to know your assignments, he did not tolerate. He then said he was going to call a few players up in front of the entire team and drill us. "Scott," he said, pointing to me, "come on up."

Oh boy, I thought, *here we go.*

"This is North Carolina lined up in the thirty nickel," Coach said, pointing to the screen. "Who's your hot read?"

"Two right side linebackers are hot, and Latrez has to break off his route," I said in an confident voice.

"Good job," Coach Friedgen said. "Sit down."

That was high praise from Ralph Friedgen.

"Nice call, Scott," Latrez Harrison said with a tap on my shoulder as I sat back down. There was a murmur of approval in the room from my teammates, a low chorus of uh-huhs and yeah mans.

A variation of my test answer was enacted in the game against the Tarheels when I had my *aha* moment reading their defense. On our opening drive, the Carolina safeties came up close to the line, and at the snap of the ball, they blitzed. I hit Latrez on a hot read slant across the middle, just like we had talked about in the film session. From that point on, I was in a groove. Everything seemed to slow down as I read the defense correctly play after play, drive after drive. My final numbers were four touchdowns passing, two touchdowns running, and 349 passing yards—Maryland 59, North Carolina 21.

Next up was a rivalry game against Virginia on a Thursday night, broadcast on ESPN. This was our senior night game, and we wanted this one badly after the Cavaliers had beaten us last season. Matt Schaub was back under center for them, and they were a quality team that none of us took lightly.

It was the coldest game I ever played in, in front of a sold-out Byrd Stadium. I had another solid game, but running back Josh Allen stole the show with thirty-eight carries for 257 yards. In the first half, Josh had an eighty-yard touchdown run, putting us up 21–7. We ended up winning the game 27–17.

Then we traveled to North Carolina State for a three-thirty game on ABC. NC State was one of those talented teams that could beat anyone or lose inexplicitly to a lesser opponent—you never knew which team was going to show—but they had been playing solid ball of late, as they had won four out of their last five games, the only loss in double overtime to Florida State. They had the great Phillip Rivers back for his senior year and a wily coach in Chuck Amato, who was an excellent defensive play caller.

During warm-ups, where both teams are on the field, stretching and running plays, Maryland went a little longer than State, which returned to their locker room. As Maryland was still in the middle of the field, the North Carolina State band appeared in the end zone and began advancing toward us. We didn't move. The drummer who was leading the band bumped into our big receiver Latrez Harrison, all 225 rock-hard pounds of him. Latrez ripped the drum out of the drummer's hands and hurled it into the stands. Boos showered down on the Maryland team, but let me tell you, that band backed up, and we finished our warm-ups. Game on. That set the tone for the day.

Carter-Finley Stadium was a full house—sixty thousand strong—and it was loud and raucous. The head referee told me before the game that if I couldn't hear to look over at him and if he thought it was too loud, he would call a time-out. If not, he would point at me to continue. I had never heard this rule, but said okay, thanks.

First play from scrimmage, standing under center, I couldn't even hear myself bark out signals. I calmly turned around and looked at the ref, and he pointed at me to continue play. The next play, I look over again as the crowd was going ballistic. I had never heard such a din. Ref pointed at me again. I never bothered looking back again, and to this day I wonder what that was all about.

The game was a dogfight from the opening whistle, and by the middle of the fourth quarter we were down 24–10, with Rivers throwing bullets all over the field. He had all the tools—six feet five and 225 pounds, with a strong arm and quick release.

And their defense used a new trick on me: they blitzed their safeties and dropped their defensive ends in coverage. It was Coach Amato's answer to me reading their safeties on blitzes and passing out quickly. At first this threw me off as they sacked me once and nearly again, but I soon made them pay by hitting my receivers on quick hitters running away from the defensive ends, who didn't have the speed to keep up.

We scored with a little under seven minutes to go, and we were down 24–17. And then with 2:29 left, I scored on a two-yard speed option play to get within one point. Inexplicably, the reliable Nick Novak missed the extra point, and we were down 24–23. The stadium was pandemonium.

We kicked off, and they ran it out to around their thirty-five yard line. The game seemed out of reach. All they had to do was keep the ball on the ground and run the clock out. On their second play, Rivers handed off to running back T. A. McLendon, and our linebacker Leroy Ambush hit T. A. with a hellacious hit under the chin, causing a fumble that Madieu Williams recovered. Unbelievable!

There was 0:35 left on the clock and still a little work for us to do in order to get Novak into field goal range. A few runs from Bruce Perry got the ball close enough, and Novak kicked a forty-three-yard field goal to redeem himself. We were now up 26–24.

But it was not over yet. With a few seconds left on the clock, North Carolina State did the lateral play on the kickoff, and when they fumbled the ball, some Maryland players ran onto the field, thinking we had won. But the ball was picked up, and eventually we downed the runner. Though a penalty could have been called, the refs signaled game over.

I was escorted toward the tunnel by two Maryland state troopers under a barrage of bottles raining down onto the field as players from both teams fought and coaches tried to separate them and get them off the field.

On the way out, I shook hands with Phillip Rivers, who was still steamed. He gave me a quick handshake and then went after an official to complain, in no uncertain terms, about the game-ending play. The stands were still packed and booing, a loud and ugly booing. It was wild!

After the game, I met Michael Tansey—our family attorney Brian Tansey's fourteen-year-old son—outside the locker room. He said to me, "I never quit believing in you coming back, Scott." It turned out that the rest of the family had left in the fourth quarter when we were down two scores to tailgate in the parking lot while Michael stuck it out in the stands.

And one last note about that game: in the four years that Phillip Rivers played for North Carolina State, he never beat Maryland. Every other team in the ACC he defeated, including Florida State twice.

The last game of the season was at Wake Forest, and we finished it off with a win, 41–28. Bruce Perry, who was constantly fighting injuries, came back with a big game, rushing for 237 yards and three touchdowns. And I was in my wheelhouse, twelve for twenty-two passing for 198 yards and three touchdown passes, and I also completed a pass to Bruce Perry for a two-point conversion.

After two seasons of running Coach Friedgen's offense, I knew the system inside and out. Coach even mentioned in an interview that it was a shame I wasn't coming back for another season, since I had a real handle on running his pro-style offense.

Brian King and I after Gator Bowl

CHAPTER 14

FULL CIRCLE

We had completed another successful season: 6–2 in the ACC and 9–3 overall. My two-year record to this point was 20–6, including the Peach Bowl win. Not bad for a quarterback nobody wanted a few years back. But I wasn't done, wanting badly to get to 21–6 in whatever upcoming bowl we were picked to play in.

There had been talk and predictions for a few weeks, but nothing was set in stone until Coach Friedgen announced at a team meeting that we were going to play in the Gator Bowl in Jacksonville, Florida, on New Years Day 2004 against the West Virginia Mountaineers on national television in front of an NBC audience.

Not only did I feel like Maryland had their number since we had beaten them three times in a row since I transferred, but it was also a chance to play my last college game with my best friends on the field at the same time. Some of them were on my Maryland team, and some of them were on the other side of the ball, playing for the Mountaineers. What more could I ask for? It was like a monster pickup game, my own field of dreams.

I had made so many friends over the last five years, and to have them all on the field with me for my final college game was something special. The media, along with everyone else, tried to make this game Scott McBrien vs. Rich Rod, but it wasn't about that for me. At this point in my college career I had no hard feelings toward Coach Rodriguez. I had already taken out that frustration the previous season. I considered my first time back in Morgantown, when we trounced West Virginia 48–17, as my payback game.

I wasn't Coach Rodriguez's biggest fan, but I had come to respect the method to his madness. In fact, I was thankful that he'd thought I couldn't play quarterback for the Mountaineers. It was the best thing he could have ever done for me. Back in fall camp when I was nursing my groin injury, Coach Friedgen and I had been standing on the sidelines, watching practice, and he said to me, "Do you think you would have developed like this at West Virginia?" I had just smiled.

Things happen for a reason. It's just that I didn't figure out what that reason was until later in my college career.

The Gator Bowl was an important game for Maryland. It was not only a chance to win another bowl game but also a chance for us to have another ten-win season and become one of only five teams in the nation to win thirty games in the last three years. The other teams were all storied programs: Louisiana State, Ohio State, Miami, Oklahoma, and Texas. We were in the same company as five elite programs led by superstar coaches such as Steve Spurrier, Mack Brown, and Nick Saban.

We spent a week in Jacksonville with practice each day, along with meetings and a different event each day. Like last year's Peach Bowl, these events included fan luncheons, charity events, hospital visits, and field trips. Much of it was fun, but all of it was time consuming, a bit of *been there, done that*. Bowls found a way to take up every single minute of our days during bowl week, and it was a grind and one reason that some teams folded come game time. We had five days of practice, events, and dinners, and then we were expected to keep our focus one last time and play a game on national television. It was not easy. But our opponent faced the same challenge.

Our hotel was in Jacksonville Landing, a huge complex of hotels, restaurants, clubs, and even a historic museum that was situated on the water. During the latter part of the week, the team had no events planned after practice, and Coach Friedgen gave us the night off. Bruce Perry, Steve Suter, Jafar Williams, and I decided to walk to a restaurant-bar with a view of the water. The place was nearly empty, and I thought that was fine. After all the hoopla of the different events, this was great.

We'd been in there for a couple of minutes when the place was stormed by a mob of West Virginia fans, all dressed to the hilt in Mountaineer sweatshirts, ball caps, jackets. It was like an invasion of loud hillbillies down from the mountains. They were everywhere, packed in booths, swarming the bar, ordering rounds of beer and shots. I hoped they didn't notice me, for fear that it could get ugly.

Then a group at the bar began singing—more like shouting—"Take Me Home, Country Road."

> *Almost heaven, West Virginia*
> *Blue ridge mountains, Shenandoah river*
> *Life is old there, older than the trees*
> *Country roads, take me home*
> *To the place I belong*
> *West Virginia, mountain momma*
> *Take me home, country roads*

I was getting nervous, but my teammates thought it was funny. Still nobody had recognized me. After a couple of minutes, I thought I might get out of there under the radar. But then a group at the bar recognized me and began chanting the name of the Mountaineer's starting quarterback, "Rasheed … Marshall, Rasheed … Marshall." I told my teammates that this chant was directed at me. Jafar said we couldn't just sit there and take it. He stood up and began chanting, "Scott … McBrien, Scott … McBrien …" Steve and Bruce got right up there with him and joined in.

Back and forth it went: *Rasheed … Marshall* and then *Scott … McBrien.* I wasn't sure where this would end up. In a fight? With someone getting hurt? Or with all of us suspended for the game?

After the chanting finally ended, to my surprise, about twenty West Virginia fans came over to the table and asked me to sign their jerseys, and some posed with me for a picture.

We finished our meal and got out of there. It would only take one drunk fan to turn things around with another chant: "F … McBrien, F … McBrien." And then who knew what might happen with my teammates, who were protective of me, their quarterback.

I was sharp all week in practice, hitting receivers in stride and play faking and running a bootleg around end, and I knew the game plan inside and out. I had watched hours of film on the Mountaineers and already knew their personnel like the back of my hand. In fact, I knew what their defense was going to do before they did.

Charlie Taaffe and Coach Friedgen did a great job of preparing us for this game. Like all the other games against West Virginia, I wasn't allowed to talk to the media. I never understood that. It wasn't like I was some hothead that was going to ramble and give them bulletin board material. I know the coaches were worried that I would say something that could be misconstrued and twisted by the other team. But anyway, no big deal.

The last day of practice we had a tradition where the seniors were carried off the practice field and could choose any two underclassmen to perform the chore. I chose Shawn Merriman and D'Qwell Jackson—both soon to become Pro Bowl NFL players. At the time they were young standout linebackers, and we used to go at it every day at practice. We had trash talked each other from the start of camp until the last practice of the season. I used to get the best of them, and I wanted to make sure I put a stamp on it and have them carry me off the field as a symbol of what I'd done to them over the last two years. But really I was thankful for going against those two stud athletes. They made me a better player by pushing me to be the best quarterback I could be. I like to think I made them better as well. That's what it was all about—competition to better ourselves.

By game day, I wasn't nervous. I had experience on my side. Nothing changed because it was a bowl game. To me it was just another game, and that's how I approached it.

Except for limited contact, Coach Friedgen had us practice like we normally did—same routine as during the season. The pregame itineraries and schedules were the same, the walk-through was identical, the interviews were the same, save me not talking with the press.

The game day weather was perfect. Not a cloud in the sky and 70 degrees. It doesn't get any better than that on January 1. Though not nervous, I was anxious to get to kickoff. It had been a long month, and we were all sick of practicing against each other.

I had family and friends who had traveled down to Jacksonville for the game. Among them were a handful of close friends; my mother; Katie—who was now a student at Maryland; Maplewood coaches Uncle

Joe Morris, Pat Meyers, and Joe La Pietra; and Brian Tansey, the attorney who had helped get my release from West Virginia.

Not only did I make their trip worthwhile, but I managed to have a career day. I felt like I could complete any pass I wanted to throw. I was as confident and comfortable as I had ever been in my college career. Seeing my old buddies on the other side of the field was awesome. They talked to me the entire game. It was trash talk, but it was fun, competitive talk. Every time I came up to the line of scrimmage, guys were talking to me: "Throw the ball my way, Scott" and "Scott, we're coming for ya" and "Don't run my way, Scott." My response to it all was a simple wink and smile before I got under center to call the cadence. Little did they know that instead of bothering me, it allowed me to think of it as playing ball in the backyard with my buddies.

The game went like the previous ones against the Mountaineers. We dominated. And the play of the game that pretty much summed up the day was a pass to the slot receiver Steve Suter—my go-to guy and a heck of a player who would have gone pro if it weren't for the knee injuries.

I threw the ball as far as I could to a covered Suter, who was streaking down the sideline. Steve had one hand being held by the defensive back, so he had to bat the ball to himself with his free hand and then went up into the air while freeing his held hand and made a one-handed catch. It was a difficult play that he made look easy.

It was simply one of those days for our team. We ended up winning the game 41–7, and my final stats were twenty one for thirty-one for 381 yards with three touchdown passes and a touchdown run. Without question, I played the game of my life.

After the final whistle, many of the West Virginia players shook my hand and congratulated me on a great game. Coach Rodriguez even came up to me and said congratulations on a heck of a season and career. That was a memorable moment for me. As I was wrapped up in handshakes and conversations, our media relations guy, Greg Creese, told me that I had won the offensive MVP trophy. At first it didn't even register with me. I was still on a high from the game.

And it turned out that the defensive MVP was my good friend for the Mountaineers, Brian King, who had made tackles all over the field.

It was very cool that we both ended our college careers winning MVPs on the same field but for different teams.

Winning the MVP was the icing on the cake. I was happy for my teammates and coaches and fans that we won, but I was also happy about winning an MVP in my last college game against my former teammates and the former coach who hadn't thought I was good enough. It was a special accomplishment for me after all that I had been through over the last five years. I guess you could say I rode off into the sunset.

And looking back on it now, it was as though providence had been at my side all during my career as a quarterback. Right from the beginning at Maplewood, under the watchful tutelage of Uncle Joe, Pat Meyers, and Joe LaPietra, through high school with fine coaches and leaders Chris Baucia and Bill McGregor, and even the bumpy times at West Virginia, I saw it all through—the good and the bad—and grew to become a better man because of it. And to get a chance to play at the University of Maryland, which I had dreamed about since my Maplewood days, was a dream come true. There wasn't a better feeling in the world than to have represented my local university and to have worn the school colors and played and won for a great coaches and good men like Mike Locksley, Charlie Taaffe, and Ralph Friedgen. I was and will always be a Terp!

EPILOGUE

After my playing days at Maryland, I had the opportunity to try out for the Green Bay Packers and get to know Brett Favre—a great guy—and play in NFL Europe and the Canadian Football League.

Those few years of playing professionally after graduating were a once-in-a-lifetime experience, but none of it compared to what it meant to be able to play for my hometown college, the University of Maryland Terrapins. Having a successful career as a Terp football player provided a launching pad for a successful business career in a major market—the Washington, DC, metropolitan area.

Being a former Maryland player not only helps me with many of my clients who are sport fans, but since 2013 I have been a color analyst on the radio for Maryland football alongside Tim Strachan and broadcasting legend Johnny Holliday. And since 2014, I have provided color commentary for Big Ten Network football games. Staying at home and playing for the Terps opened doors that wouldn't have been possible anywhere else.

Fear the turtle!

Printed in the United States
By Bookmasters